PRAISE FOR DEFY THE BAD GUY

"I could not put this book down! Every page has practical advice that I felt I could use, which every woman should know and actively follow."

-- Wendy Hoegerman, Computer Systems Analyst, Business Intelligence

"This book is the one must read for all busy women. Learning how to be mentally and physically prepared in the event of an unexpected attack is something all of us need to know how to do. DEFY the Bad Guy teaches you how to be ready for danger in simple and concise language. It has you thinking long after you've put the book down. I carry it around in my car to remind myself that danger can be lurking around every corner and if it is, I don't have to be it's victim."

--Louise Gorsica, Yorktown, VA

"Thank you Julie Greene for writing DEFY the Bad Guy. I want to thank you as a woman for helping us be safer in our daily lives. I also want to thank you as a physician who cares for victims of domestic violence and sexual assault. And most of all I want you thank you as a mother of a daughter for helping all mothers empower our daughters and keep them as safe as possible. Every mother needs to read and give a copy of DEFY the Bad Guy to her daughter, especially when her daughter starts dating and driving. Every women's college dormitory and sorority needs to give copies of this book to their new members as well."

--Caroline A. Wadlin MD, www.thepowerofpinkmd.com

"Julie Greene's DEFY the Bad Guy is "Safe and Secure 101"... This is a book that can inform and empower women (and any men who are smart enough to read and heed!) to lead a safe and fear-free life for themselves and their families. Well done, Julie!"

--Lt. Col. Dave Grossman, author of *On Killing*, which was nominated for a Pulitzer Prize, and founder of the Warrior Science Group

"DEFY the Bad Guy is a book that every woman and girl MUST read. I have my 9 year old daughter reading it, for there are so many great tips that she can learn and use as of right now. As a woman, we can never be too safe, and Julie has written it in an awesome way, where it can simply benefit anyone who reads it!"

--Zohra Sarwari, International Speaker/Author/Coach, www.MuslimWomanSpeaker.com

"DEFY the Bad Guy is a comprehensive book jam-packed full of personal protection strategies, tips, tricks, advice, and resources for today's "every" woman. I recommend every woman owns one."

--Susan Stevenson, Diplomatic Protection Services United and International Combat Hapkido Federation of New Zealand

"Julie's commitment to self defense training is second only to her passion to help others. This is evidenced by her latest work; upon completion of this book the reader will be empowered, aware, and ready to DEFY the Bad Guy."

- Master Mark S. Gridley, President Life Protection Arts & Sciences, Director of Anatomical Targeting Strategies

"DEFY the Bad Guy is such an easy read and gives great tips on how to keep your wits and survive an attack. Bravo Julie for writing such an incredibly helpful book for women! I am looking forward to the Audible.com version!"

--Tricia Tinnon, co-owner, Action Arts Academy, USA, 2nd Degree WTF Taekwondo

"The strength of DEFY the Bad Guy lies in the strategy for creating a mindset that will help you avoid dangerous situations."

--Sgt. Sanford Strong, author, *Strong on Defense*

"DEFY the Bad Guy starts with the author's story and engages the reader, providing manageable and down-to-earth steps every woman can take to avoid violence and be confidently safe."

--James Malinchak, Co-Author, *Chicken Soup for the College Soul*, "2-Time College Speaker of the Year!" founder, www.BigMoneySpeaker.com

"This book is a must-read if you are concerned about you and your family's safety. It is packed full of safety tips and preventative strategies that you can easily incorporate into your daily life."

--Julie Morrison, Speaker, Author of *Cut Past Your Competition*

DEFY the Bad Guy is an excellent addition to any women's self-defense library. In it you will find practical advice regarding the violence that permeates today's society and how to deal with it."

--Master John Scali, owner and instructor of Self-Defense America Club and Vice President of the International Combat Hapkido

DEFY
The Bad Guy

Powerful Practical Self-Defense
Strategies for Every Woman

by Julie Greene

Second Edition
Julie Greene Personal Safety Solutions

Published by Julie Greene Personal Safety Solutions

Copyright © 2010 by Julie Greene Personal Safety Solutions

Second Edition

Printed in the United States of America

Greene, Julie

Defy the Bad Guy: *Powerful Practical Self-Defense Strategies for Every Woman*

ISBN: 978-0-9823997-0-5

Photo by Patti Brown Photography
Cover Design and Layout by James Arrington

Disclaimer/Warning

This book is full of good ideas that the reader can use for making decisions about personal safety. It is created to provide authoritative and useful information derived from the author's personal experience and research. It is a reference book, not a self-defense handbook. It is also not a substitute for legitimate training or emergency assistance. The author/publisher makes no promises of surviving an attack using this information. After reading this book, the author/publisher strongly suggests professional hands-on self-defense training. The application of this information may be demanding for the reader and it is recommended that the reader consult a health care provider or physician prior to beginning training.

How the reader uses this information is at their discretion. The suggested preventative measures and responsive techniques may not be effective in all situations, as a criminal, especially a person committing a violent crime, will be unpredictable. The author/publisher does not assume any responsibility for the use/misuse of information in this book. This includes injury or damage to the reader or to any other person or loss incurred after using or applying, either indirectly or directly, any method described in this book.

Certain self-defense practices described in this book may not be justified in every particular situation or under local, federal, or state law. The author/publisher makes no warranty or representation regarding the legality of any technique illustrated in this book. The author/publisher is not engaged in providing legal or any other professional service and does not accept any form of liability.

Resource information such as contact information, websites, and phone numbers were correct at the time this book went to press. Please contact Feedback@ DEFYTheBadGuy.com if you discover incorrect contact information.

If you do not wish to be bound by the above, you may return this book to the author for a full refund.

This book is dedicated to every woman on the planet who needs to know how to live in safety.

TABLE OF CONTENTS

ACKNOWLEDGEMENTS

It is a challenge writing a book for the first time. I cannot even try to cite all of the sources and authorities consulted as I prepared the text of this book. That list includes many individuals, websites, libraries, and departments of the federal government.

I have many thanks of appreciation to my teachers, Master Brad Tinnon and all of the instructors at Action Arts Academy, USA, Grandmaster John Pellegrini, Master David Rivas, Master Mark Gridley, and instructor Doug Boyd of the International Combat Hapkido Federation, and the fine instructors at R.A.D. Systems.

Lots of love to my training buddies, Amazing Michelle, Crackerjack Carmen, and Superhero Sheri.

To my editor, Supersonic Susie, you know we will be going places.

To my friend and fellow author Generous Julie, thank you for your inspiration and support.

To my Miraculous Mom, a true survivor in more ways than one, to my son, Magnificent Morgan, who has spent hours practicing with me since he was seven, and to my husband Genius George, who has patiently supported my training and honey, I promise, I will never bend your fingers back that far again!

FOREWORD

You hold in your hands an outstanding reference guide to personal safety.

I was intrigued when Julie sent me an advance copy of this book. She was looking for a testimonial, but after reading it I insisted on writing the Foreword. This is the book that I planned on writing for women's protection. She has just beaten me to the metaphorical punch.

Self-protection is a fundamental right of every being on the planet. The misunderstood part of that right is the understanding that you must take control of your own protection—as you are responsible for yourself and no one is coming to help you. Your interest in this book indicates that you are on that path to this understanding and perhaps even ready to take those first steps.

Julie has written an excellent guide to assist you in that journey. The core material is presented in an easy manner that invites you to continue reading. Although the book can be finished in a few hours, you will want to keep it handy for quick reference. The content can be deceptive: it will take several readings to fully appreciate the practical advice it provides.

The strongest measure you can take in personal safety is avoidance. As a tactic, this not as sexy as a jumping, spinning heel-kick to your attacker's temple, but it is far more effective. Unlike a complicated kick, avoidance is something that anyone of any age and physical ability can practice. It is a theme that is stressed and repeated throughout this book and one of the reasons I recommend it so strongly. In martial arts the best block is not to be there. Similarly, in personal protection, the best defense to a criminal attack is to avoid the conflict all together.

The partner to avoidance is awareness. In order to avoid trouble, you must first be aware that it even exists. This is where Julie's practical advice excels. Over half of this book is about becoming aware of where threats may lie. Once you identify trouble spots, you can avoid them.

Once you incorporate Julie's tips and techniques, you will move through your daily routine in a far safer manner. You will still shop at the local grocery store, use the Internet to buy fun gadgets, and drop your children at school. But there will be a difference. You will subconsciously check for problem areas and subtly adjust your patterns to avoid trouble. In the self-protection industry, we call this being in Condition Yellow, relaxed and alert. This is the place you want to be and Julie can guide you there.

Welcome to an eye-opening read that will help you live a safer life.

Alex Haddox
President, Palladium Education, Inc.
Host of the Practical Defense podcast

Chapter 1

Introduction

Self defense is Nature's oldest law – John Dryden

It's dark out. You've been shopping and you've got to get from the building to your car parked in the lot. You have so many things on your mind. Did you get everything done? Where are you going next? Who is waiting for you to come home or to pick them up? Where are your keys? How do you search for your keys and hang on to these bags at the same time? Scanning the parking lot, you try to remember where your car is parked. You get that jittery, scared feeling as you begin to navigate between the cars. Ugh. You hate walking alone here. You don't even want to think what can happen. You see a man walking by himself in the next lane. You don't know him. Is he coming toward you? Why did that van park so close to your car? Will you make it to your car safely? What would happen if that guy got too close, or if someone was in that van watching you? You are very nervous and a little freaked out, so you hurry to unlock your car, get in where you'll be safe, and quickly drive away.

Now imagine that you're at home. It's evening. The kids are in bed and you just turned out the light. You hear a noise downstairs. It sounds like glass breaking, but you're not sure. You think someone is in your house. What do you do? What can you do?

Now imagine you're working late. Everyone in the office has gone home. You have just one more thing to finish before you can go. One of your new clients shows up and comes into your office, shutting the door behind him. You tell him that it's past closing time and ask him to come back tomorrow. He says he has only one question, and it won't take long; he promises that he will leave. You pack up your stuff and head for the closed door, all of a sudden feeling like you've got to get out of there, NOW.

How many times have you been in situations like these where you've been concerned about your safety? For many women, it's every day, sometimes several times in the day. You get that fearful feeling in the pit of your stomach or feel the stress in your shoulders. You have heard the stories of women who have been assaulted, abducted, raped, or murdered, caught alone in the parking lot or walking down the street in an unfamiliar neighborhood. Every woman worries about these situations. There could be someone waiting in any of these places, wanting to hurt you. If you are alone, you are often uncomfortable and very likely scared.

Statistics tell the story

These are not unfounded fears. In 2007, the United States Department of Justice statistics stated that there were approximately 23 million crimes committed against people living in this country who were age 12 and older. Of those crimes, 17.5 million were property crimes, theft and burglary. Over five million of those crimes were violent crimes, robbery, assault, and rape. About 250,000 of those crimes were sexual assault, and that number is up by 25% from 190,000 in 2005. In one year, that's one in 1000 people, mostly women, who will experience a completed or attempted rape. According to the National Violence Against Women Survey, one in six women (other studies report one in three) reported experiencing a completed or an attempted rape at some time in their lives, and that doesn't count the unreported crimes (some studies estimate that only about 16% of assaults are reported).

Denial won't make it go away

Imagine yourself again in that parking lot, office, or upstairs at home. What can you do? Could you get away? Could you fight? Would you fight? Or would you freeze? Usually, a woman will respond one of two ways. One is, "I just hope it never happens to me." This is denial, and it ain't a river in Egypt. The reality, documented by the Department of Justice statistics and one in three-to-six women you know, is that you can hope all you want, but you may still find yourself in a violent situation.

The other response is to think that you can rely on your boyfriend, husband, the police, or whatever good guy is around to protect you. Unfortunately, these guys are not with you everywhere you go. For obvious reasons, the bad guy prefers to commit crimes when his chosen victim is alone. Think of all of the times when you are by yourself, when you are going to and from work, classes, or shopping, where there are no known good guys in sight. It's just you. *You need to be responsible for your own safety.*

Who is the "bad guy"?

Let's talk for a moment about the "bad guy." In actuality, the bad guy can be either a man or a woman, but since most violence against women is done by men, we're going to call our aggressor the bad *guy.* This bad guy is often likely to be someone you know, but also might be a random stranger. He is someone who doesn't care if he harms you and may want to cruelly and maliciously hurt you. Let's also define "hurts you" as not just harming your physical body, but inflicting mental harm and/or emotional harm as well. Simply put, the bad guy is someone who does not respect you or your wishes, and he will callously harm you to get what he wants.

Just so you know, I'm not male-bashing here by any means. I am so thankful for all of the good guys out there. Fortunately, they are the majority of the population! I speak for all women when I say that their contribution to our safety is greatly appreciated.

You can protect yourself

It is possible for you to protect yourself and your family from violence. Sanford Strong, in his book, *Strong on Defense*, tells the story of a family who encountered intruders armed with knives while camping. Four criminals confronted the husband, teenage son, and daughter and ordered them face down on the ground. Wondering where everybody was, Mom came out of the camper. Quickly assessing the situation, she immediately became angry at the criminals who were threatening to harm her family. She refused when the bad guys told her to lie down and instead went straight for them, furious and determined to make them let her family go. She stayed on her feet, hitting and yelling from the center of her being, as they fought back with their knives. Yet her resistance enabled the other family members to escape from the aggressors and fight back, eventually driving the intruders away. The mom was injured and got cut, but she survived and ensured the survival of her family.

I pray that you will never have to experience an encounter like the woman in the story. However, like her, you inherently have just about everything you need to avoid and survive a violent encounter. You have passion for the people that you love and when you add some effective strategies and techniques, you will be able to channel that passion into action that can save your life and the lives of people you care about.

See yourself as a superhero. In the movies, a "normal" person becomes a superhero when something supernatural is added to the regular self. Well, most of you are "normal," and fortunately, you don't have to have a spider bite you or be contaminated with chemicals to access your powers. Instead, you're going to add some common-sense ideas (which may seem supernatural) and create some new responses to scary situations. These will be your Superpowers of Safety. In this book, I'm going to talk about how you can train your brain to incorporate these "Superpowers" into your everyday thinking and living.

No Guarantee

Unlike movie or television superheroes, however, there is no guarantee that what you will learn, even after years of self-defense study, will enable you to vanquish every bad guy in every situation, every time. However, by taking immediate and effective action, you increase your chances for survival by many, many times and lower the risk of anything ever happening at all.

The Three "P's" of Personal Safety

There are three basic types of Superpowers that will help you survive in a bad situation. They are Prevention, Perception, and Power. Think of them as layers of personal safety, one building upon the other for your greatest self-defense success.

Prevention

The outer layer is that of Prevention, your invisible shield. The best defense against a violent encounter is to make sure that it is hard work for the bad guy to get to you. He needs access to his victim and a place where he can commit his crime quietly, quickly, and without being seen. He is always on the watch for situations where he can do this. The goal of Prevention is that he never even sees you as a possible victim. Or, if he does see you, he may consider you as a victim for a moment, but then reconsider and move on. (I do hope that as more women learn and practice personal safety habits, he will have a hard time finding *anyone* to victimize and will decide to change careers and become a useful person in society.)

With the Power of Prevention, your goal is to set up barriers that will make the bad guy bypass you because it is too much work to get to you. This book will cover preventive measures you can take in the parking lot, at home, and in your car. The Power of Safe Journey will cover safety while traveling.

Perception

The Power of Awareness and the Power of Intuition are two powers that are included in the second "P", Perception. Peripheral, or outer, Perception is about becoming aware of the area around you. Awareness can be practiced, and I'll show you how. If the bad guy, for whatever reason, decides you may be worth the trouble, you can employ these strategies that will help you notice when he is coming near you. Practiced breathing techniques can help calm you as you assess the situation.

Personal (inner) Perception helps you tune in to your intuition, listen to your fear signals, and learn when to act on them. The Power of Boundaries gives you some great techniques to defend the shield you've erected. Perception will help you become aware of the guy next to you and help you determine whether he's a good guy or not.

Power

The innermost layer of the three P's is Power. The Power of Voice encompasses how you hold your body and how you use your voice to create and defend your boundaries. The Power of Escape will include powerful techniques to help you get away. With the Power of Angry Attack, you will learn how to employ the most effective ways to strike an assailant. You can also use the Power of Visualization to help train your subconscious for a successful encounter with an aggressor. You will find that with practice, you will have the power to defend yourself.

I know the sexiest part of the whole personal safety thing is learning how to smack the bad guy to submission. I mean, what woman doesn't fantasize about delivering a devastating kick to the bad guy's family jewels and seeing him writhe on the ground in pain after he's tried to hurt you? Well, first, if it gets to that, don't stick around long enough to watch; get the heck away from there to a safe, populated spot and call the police.

Second, before you flip directly to the techniques in the back, read through the first part of the book, particularly the Prevention section, and set up as many barriers to the bad guy as you can. Then read and practice the techniques in the Perception section so you can train yourself to listen to intuition, be aware, and define and enforce boundaries. This will develop early warning signals that will help you get out of there before trouble starts happening. You really don't want circumstances to escalate to that groin-kicking point. Only then, when you are unable to remove yourself from an ugly situation and have no other choice but to get him out of your way so you can escape, will you employ the physical techniques.

So, let's get going!

*In any situation, ask yourself: What strengths do I possess
that can contribute towards accomplishing something in
this situation? Then follow through.*

– Source unknown

Chapter 2
Develop Your Hidden Powers of Self-Defense

The mind is like a trunk: if it is well packed, it holds almost everything; if ill-packed, next to nothing.

– Augustus William Hare and Julius Charles Hare

Welcome to the wonderful world of self-defense! Before we get into practical techniques and exercises for your personal safety, I want to talk about how your physical system of brain and body gets from sitting pretty and minding your own business to facing an aggressor and defending yourself. When you are comfortable and relaxed, you are generally not restricted in any way. Your heartbeat and breathing are regular, you can see and hear what is happening around you, and you can do cool things like tie your shoelaces or dial your insurance company's phone number, sometimes both at the same time.

Your Automatic Stress Reaction

When you are afraid, however, your subconscious brain and body have their own program, no matter what the rest of you thinks about it. When you are facing, or even merely anticipating, some kind of scary situation, whether it is asking for a raise, giving a speech, or fighting off a rapist, changes occur in your body that you cannot control. Your heart rate goes up and blood rushes from your extremities to the large muscle groups (forget about the shoelaces or dialing that phone number). You can't hear anything but the most important sounds and your vision decreases peripherally and focuses to only what is set straight in front of you. It's harder to breathe. All of these things happen automatically.

The brain, as it has done since cavewoman times, narrows your behavior choices to "flight or fight." In the good old days, when we were hunters and gatherers rather than computer programmers and dog walkers, this reaction was very useful to our survival. The increase in heart rate meant that blood was forcefully pumped to large muscles like those in our legs, the better for us to run or fight with. Intensified visual and aural focus meant that we could see and hear that saber-toothed tiger coming at us. Perspiration increased to cool the body in preparation for the hot job of sprinting away. All thoughts flew out of our head except for those that accessed our spear-throwing or child-protecting skills for survival.

Would you really choose to sweat?

In it's infinite wisdom, your body knows enough not to trust your thinking brain to decide when to activate these survival functions. It delegates this job to your subconscious brain. Your stress reaction happens automatically. Who has not felt this when you stand up in front of a group of people to speak or when you thought you lost your kid in the grocery store? Heart beating out of your chest, shaking hands (blood flows from hands to larger muscle groups), and sweating in places you didn't think could sweat. That's the cavewoman stress response.

Of course, you've seen this reaction in animals, the "deer in the headlights" response. The deer will automatically run from familiar dangers, but is frozen in the road because there's nothing in its subconscious about how to deal with an oncoming car. However, its muscles are tensed in preparation for a quick escape.

I always get a kick out of watching my little cat go into stress response when he's threatened by the big cat. Even though I've never measured his heartbeat, I can see his arched back, tail up, hair on end. He stands light on his feet, ready for action. Lord knows what's going on in that brain of his, but you can sure see the focus on his target and hear his hiss of warning. He can spring directly to counter the attack from the big cat or zip away behind the china cabinet, his favorite safe zone. And it all happens in the subconscious "instinctual" part of his brain.

Your brain needs input

Unlike my little cat, who practices fighting daily with the big cat, I'll bet most of you have grown up never learning how to fight. You also have probably never even practiced running from someone who is trying to hurt you. In a dangerous or scary situation, your body will have the shaky-hand-physical-stress response. When your brain searches for spear-throwing, escape, or some similar defense response, it finds nothing. There is nothing to work with in the case of a possible violent encounter, so you "freeze."

Your brain needs some kind of data and experience to refer to when a violent encounter occurs. Ideally, that experience would be hands-on and practiced regularly until it is part of your muscle memory. But studies have shown that even just imagining yourself succeeding in a situation can be valuable as well. Some people use the analogy of your brain as a file cabinet. You fill each file with information that your brain can access in a given situation. I'd like to change the analogy to something that you all carry with you. Instead of the file cabinet, let's say the place where your go-to safety information is stored is in the wallet in your purse.

Create your Superpower Wallet

Think about it. Your brain is like your wallet. You always carry it with you. You keep some of your most important items in it. Do you know where your wallet is right now? Of course you do. It carries important information and items you need. Do you know what is in your wallet? You can probably picture the inside of your wallet and have a good idea of what's in there. What happens if you want to buy something and your wallet is empty? No sale, right? Without your money, checkbook, or credit cards, you "freeze" and can't complete the transaction. Your brain works the same way. So when you are in a situation that elicits the automatic stress reaction, it is as if you are going shopping without anything in your wallet. You "freeze" because your brain, like the empty wallet you carry, does not have the information, or currency, it needs to deal with a possible violent encounter or stressful situation. You need to create a Superpower Wallet, a space in your brain filled with information on how to be safe and deal with different violent encounters, and carry it with you everywhere you go.

Let's shop for your Superpower Wallet. In your mind's eye, imagine you're at the Superpower Wallet store. Look at all the Wallets on the shelf. Pick one out. It needs to be big and it needs to be pretty. Maybe it has nature scenes, pictures of your family, or the words "Goddess of Beauty" on it. Look at all the choices until you see the one that is perfect for you. Pick it up and open it to see that it has enough room for everything you will need to keep you safe.

Now you have a place to store your Superpowers of Safety, the Wallet where your subconscious will go when it's stressed. You can fill your Wallet with what you learn and practice in order to be safe and prepared for an emergency. When you are safe, you feel confident, more independent, and secure. You have tools that you can use to protect yourself, your home, and your family. Your Wallet will contain the knowledge of how to use your senses to alert yourself to danger. When danger arrives, you access it for options to use to get you and your family safe. I'm not saying that you'll be able to go from a little knowledge of self-defense to using fancy moves to nail the guy right away, but you can be more prepared when the situation arises. That will greatly lower your risk of getting hurt.

One caveat: please understand that this information does not take the place of a hands-on self-defense course. It is possible to spend days, weeks, and years learning self-defense and practicing different ways to physically get away from or attack someone. I emphatically recommend that you follow up on the information in this book with a self-defense class or some kind of training and I'll give you some of my favorite suggestions later in the book.

When you practice self-defense skills in a safe environment, especially when you have the opportunity to take your best shots on a scary guy in a padded suit, you provide your subconscious with valuable information it can use in a dangerous situation. However, until you can make a commitment to attend some kind of training, you can begin to think differently when you're in that parking lot or walking down the street. Begin to fill the Wallet of your subconscious with the Superpowers of Safety. When you have a Wallet chock full of ideas, techniques, and experiences that will help you avoid violence, you will have a better idea of what your options are and how to execute them when you need to.

From no defense to self-defense

So how did a (muffled sound)-year old mom get into the self-defense business? Working to make women stronger has been an interest of mine for a long time. I grew up with a father who was an unpredictable alcoholic. According to dad, I was fat and stupid; even though I had straight A's and was captain of the girls volleyball team. I watched him berate my mom about almost everything, and remember lying in bed at night listening to them argue in their room next door, feeling helpless.

When I moved away from home, I swore to myself that no way in hell would I ever find myself in a situation like that again. In fact, it became my passion to learn how to show other women and girls how to avoid or escape abusive situations as well. I volunteered at the local women's shelter, answering the Hotline and being available for the women there. I read books which helped me understand how to make myself stronger and believe in myself. Going physical, I took a four-week Rape Aggression Defense (R.A.D.) self-defense course. It was fun learning how to kick and punch. I felt so powerful for a few weeks. But life goes on, and soon after that I was pregnant with my son, Morgan. I guess I never fully realized that having a child would be so life-changing.

Those of you with children know that your life is never the same after they are born. You find yourself doing and saying things that you never imagined when you were childfree. Sentences come out of your mouth like "don't eat the dinosaurs" or "take the gerbils out of the bathtub." When my son was seven, we went to a children's festival and saw a demonstration of kung fu. They had cool uniforms, used weapons, and jumped high. The kid was impressed, so we enrolled him in Taekwondo class. After three months of watching, I joined the class, too.

Taekwondo is a Korean martial art which has evolved into a competitive sport. You put some padding around your midsection and earn points by kicking your opponent, aiming for one of the targets painted on his padding. All the while, he is trying to kick you. It's basically a game with very strict rules aimed at keeping the participant's body parts intact and non-bleeding while points are being scored. In the dojang where we were training, we would play this kicking game that they call sparring, barely touching each other to learn control.

After about a year of practicing sparring with very little contact, I was feeling pretty confident about the whole thing, actually rather indestructible. Then one day, sparring with a young man, I got kicked hard. HARD, as in knock-the-air-out-of-me hard. In the nicest way that I could think of as I was gasping for air, I asked him to tone it down. I think the exact words were, "Please don't kick me so hard, I have to make dinner tonight." Next round, BOOM! He did it again, and then again. My need to appear tough in front of the class forced me to keep my head up until I walked out the door, even though I was pretty shaken up. However, as soon as I got into my car, I started sobbing. I cried on and off for three days straight, not really knowing what was wrong with me.

When I finally calmed down, I realized that it wasn't the pain to my body at all that got me so upset. That went away pretty quick. It was pain to my spirit, an unexpected assault. I had worked so hard all these years to become strong, and yet I still didn't have the basic stuff inside me to deal with this (admittedly mild) violent encounter. Even though I had been learning to kick and punch, I didn't know how to change my thinking to keep myself safe from the inside and how to better enforce my boundaries.

As women, I'll bet most of you were not taught how to fight and did not practice roughhousing like your brothers did when you were kids. I sure wasn't. We never had the hands-on opportunity to develop skills in response to attack. However, since the sparring incident, I have learned a few techniques that have helped me and I will share them with you. In this book I am going to show you some moves that will seriously disable anyone who wants to mess with you. However, it isn't enough just to learn how to hit someone. You need to develop the mindset to get you from minding your own business to getting out of trouble and knowing that you did your best.

You have the right and ability to protect yourself

You have the right to defend yourself. You are allowed to choose the people who get close to you and keep people away who you believe might hurt you. It is against the law for someone to touch you, follow you, and/or harass you without your permission. Even knowing that these laws are in place to protect you, in certain situations your automatic cavewoman stress response, also known as fear, will kick in when you sense danger. But realize that fear is a good thing — it's a built-in warning system. Use that warning to alert yourself to take action; action that is needed to get you out of a dangerous situation.

You have the ability to defend yourself. You can employ strategies that will keep you away from violence and away from the bad guy. Ideally, the perfect self-defense scenario is where NOTHING HAPPENS because you kept the danger away. If you do encounter the bad guy, you can use your brain, parts of your body (the sharp, hard, poky ones), and your spirit and passion to get yourself safe. You have the power to do this.

This is where the 3 P's of Personal Safety come into play. **Prevention** is about creating habits and systems that will make the bad guy want to pass you by. If he gets closer, employ **Perception** by practicing awareness and using your intuition to keep him away and defuse the situation if he's close. If you determine he is a bad guy and he engages you, it's time for **Power**. Use the power of your stance, your voice, and your body to escape. If you can't escape, then it's time to harness the power of your stress response. Get angry, strike powerfully, explosively, and with intention until you can get away safely.

My mission

I have this vision that every woman will realize the power she has to prevent crime and protect herself and her family from physical and emotional harm. If more women used even a few of the options in this book, I believe that there would be less violence in the world, as the bad guys would find it too difficult to assault us. Women would learn how to be "hard" targets, not easy targets for these bad guys. Our subconscious would be ready with preventive strategies and hands-on techniques. These strategies and techniques would be practiced until they become instinctual. What a wonderful world it will be when a woman won't be freaked out every time she walks down the street or enters a parking lot because she knows what to do to keep herself safe. I invite you to join me in making this vision a reality.

Oh, one more thing. Throughout this book, I'm going to give you "do's", not "don'ts." Rather than trying to remember what NOT to do, it will be easier to learn and remember what you *need* to do. Stay positive and let's start to fill your Wallet with your Superpowers.

I'm not afraid of storms, for I'm learning to sail my ship.

– Louisa May Alcott

Chapter 3

Your Invisible Shield
The Power of Prevention

*You cannot prevent the birds of sorrow from flying over your head,
but you can prevent them from building nests in your hair.*

– Chinese proverb

One of my favorite superhero powers in the movies is the force field. It is usually made of some kind of mysterious energy particles that create an indestructible bubble around the person who uses it. This bubble keeps intruders out and repels attacks. I've noticed that this power, instead of the turning-into-a-green-hulk power, is mostly employed by superhero women. I guess it's probably because they can still keep their clothes nice when they're using it.

You can create your own invisible shields that keep the bad guy away from you. These protective shields work everywhere you go: in your home, in your car, and when you're in transit from one place to another.

The first "P" of Personal Safety: Prevention

The following Prevention tips will help you build your force field and can be placed in your Superpower Wallet. Many of these tips will be familiar. You've heard them from your mom, television, forwarded emails, and possibly your dog. However, just because they're familiar does not mean that you are using them. How many of you really lock your doors, all the time? News flash -- if you lock your doors, it is much less likely that someone uninvited will come into your house and steal from you or hurt you. Go figure.

Even though you've heard these a hundred times before, I invite you to look at these strategies with a fresh eye. Implementing them will help ensure that you have the most powerful shield possible. Go through this list and see which strategies are normal habits for you and check the boxes next to them. These are the things in your Superpower Wallet already. Hooray! Now go back and look at the empty boxes. Work on adding these strategies to your Wallet as well. Take it slow. Trying to implement every one of these all at once will just drive you crazy. How about adding just one, until it becomes habit, every week?

Usually, number one on everybody's "I think a crime will happen here" list is the parking lot or parking garage, but it can be expanded to any relatively confined area away from the general public. Much of this information below is inspired by Marc MacYoung's excellent website, www.nononsenseselfdefense.com. Let's begin with strategies for the marginal areas.

MARGINAL AREAS

Marginal areas are transitional places that border busy, noisy, and populated places. Parking lots, stairwells and elevators, ATMs, public restrooms, or any room in a house or building away from where people are can be considered marginal areas. In and of themselves, they are not inherently dangerous. You probably pass through a marginal area at least once or twice every day to get where you want to go. People in a marginal area are there to do one specific thing, such as get to their car in a parking lot, go to the bathroom in the public restroom, or get to a higher or lower floor in a building. Since a marginal area like a parking lot is not your prime destination, you may not always pay attention to what's going on around you there. Your thoughts and energies are often focused on where you are going next. That is one of the main reasons so many crimes happen here.

The bad guy loves the marginal areas because they offer him so many opportunities. Remember, he is on the lookout for a place where he can commit a crime quickly, quietly, and unseen. In this transitional area, there are fewer people, which means he is less likely to be noticed or seen committing a crime. There are fewer people to hear him break something or hear his victim's call for help. Most importantly, he can sneak up on someone who is not paying attention to where they are because they are focused on their next destination.

Even more appealing to the bad guy is the opportunity for a quick getaway. A robbery can -- and often does -- take less than 10 seconds. In the marginal area, by the time somebody sees you, figures out what's going on, and comes over to help you, a full 30 seconds can pass. That's a huge head start for the bad guy. Ask the question, "Can anyone reach me in 30 seconds?" If the answer is yes, you know you're in a marginal area.

Any marginal area can be scary, but you can lower the freak-out factor if you know what to look for. There are two simple strategies you can use to keep yourself safe. First, you need to be aware of what you would usually expect there. Ask yourself, "What is normal for this area?" Second, pay attention to abnormal activity. The marginal area is only dangerous when you notice something unusual going on. If you see something that raises a red flag, keep your distance, get back to a more populated place, and let somebody know what's going on.

PARKING LOT

In the parking lot, people normally go directly from their cars into the school, mall, or office. When they come from these buildings, they will go straight to their vehicle and maybe spend a little time loading their packages or children into the car before they get in and drive away. If people are waiting for someone, they are usually waiting by the entrance to the school or store, or sometimes sitting in their cars. If there is a group of people talking among themselves, they normally are all facing each other, not paying much attention to you. If there are people between cars, they are loading their packages or making a short cut to or from the entrance. These things are usual.

So what is unusual for a parking lot? People hanging around, loitering, with no visible purpose. Someone coming toward you, not toward their own car might also mean trouble. When you see unusual activity, go back to the populated area and grab some company; ideally, the security guard for the building or mall, but a trustworthy employee from one of the stores or businesses can also help you.

When you acknowledge a not-perfect situation and get some company to face it, you are the embodiment of a strong, intelligent woman. You are not a chicken or a wimp. You are also NOT, by any stretch of the imagination, "causing a scene" or "bothering people who have more important things to do." You are doing these organizations a favor. They *want* to come out and take care of it. Scary parking lots are bad for business. Here are some strategies you can use in the parking lot. Check the boxes next to the things you are already doing.

☐ While you are still inside the building, before you enter the parking lot or garage, get your keys out of your purse and hold the key that opens your car door as if you're using it to start your car. You probably are already doing this if you have a remote lock.

☐ If you have packages to carry, use a cart or make a couple of trips so you can easily manage your purchases and belongings with one hand while holding your keys in another. The extra time it takes for that second trip is well worth it to keep your key-holding hand free.

☐ If you are in the parking lot and see someone wandering aimlessly or loitering, go back inside (loop around if you have to) and get security or a store employee to keep you company as you walk to your car.

☐ A group of guys lined up against the wall, watching the parking lot and paying specific attention to you means danger. If you see a group of people not engaged primarily with each other, stay away from them, loop around and go back into the building, alert security, and have them walk you out, perhaps after they've scattered the loiterers.

☐ If you see more than one person and they split up as they head for you, get out of there immediately. Head back inside the building or toward somewhere lighted, noisy, and populated. Get company to walk you out to your car.

☐ Some parking lots or structures have a little recessed area near where people enter and exit, often near the elevators. The bad guy can stand there, not hiding, and you won't see him because you are focused on getting to your car. It is easy for him to come up behind you and ambush you if you are not paying attention. He chooses to be in plain sight because if he is hiding behind something, it is harder for him to see you and jump over obstacles to reach you. Keep an eye out for these areas and if you see someone hanging out there, go back into the building and get security to walk you to your car and get rid of the bad guy. (Are you seeing a trend here? You are safer when you have company.)

☐ If you see a car pulling up next to you in the middle of the parking lot as you are heading toward your car, change direction and get into the next lane with at least one car between you and the car coming. Maybe they just want directions, but this is truly an inappropriate place to get or give information. If people need directions that bad, they can park their car and ask someone inside the building.

☐ If you see someone coming up to you as you approach your car, move away. Immediately walk around your car so that you have a car between you, go back into the building, and get company. I'll talk about what you can do when you are confronted in Chapter 5.

☐ As you're walking toward your car, from enough distance away, take a glance underneath. No need to get down on your knees and stick your face under there. Take a glance in the back seat before you unlock the door.

☐ When you get to your car, look to see if there is someone sitting in the passenger seat of the car or van next to your driver's side. If someone's there, go back into the building and get some company. If, for some reason, company is not available, open the passenger door of your car and slide over to the driver's seat. Lock your doors after you get in.

☐ Shopping with your children? Keep your children in the cart while you load the groceries first. If there is a carjacking situation, you can leave the keys, car, and groceries, while keeping your kids with you.

☐ If you get into your car and it won't start, before you get out, first look to see if there's anybody around your car. If you see someone who might be a threat, stay in the car and call 911 for help. If not, get out of the car and go back into the building and call AAA, security, or whoever you know who will help you. DO NOT accept the help of the well-meaning stranger who "just happens" to be there.

Parking lot safety plan

Use this plan to avoid crime in this marginal area.

☐ Before you leave the building, have your key in one hand, packages in another.

☐ As you enter the parking lot, look around the entrance to the building, even behind you if there are some recessed areas.

☐ Look directly at any people waiting at the entrance.

☐ Keep an eye out behind you and around you as you walk to your car. You are not paranoid; you are calmly noting that everything is normal for that area.

☐ If you sense something unusual, like someone following you, keep walking and loop back around toward the building and get some company to walk you out.

☐ When you get to your car, check out the inside of your car and the surrounding area one more time before you unlock the door(s).

☐ If you see someone coming toward you, move to a more populated, well-lit place and get some company.

☐ Load your packages, get in, lock your doors, put on your seatbelt, and go.

☐ Save that phone call for a stop in a more populated area and balance your checkbook at home.

Elevators and Stairs

Elevators and stairs are marginal areas inside a building. Choose to take the elevator instead of the stairs. What is usual in the elevator? The same rules apply here as they do in the parking lot scenarios.

☐ If you have even the smallest "ick" feeling about someone in the elevator as you are getting in it, turn around, fake that you forgot something, and let it go up without you. Take the next one.

☐ Stand back from the elevator while you are waiting, out of anyone's reach to pull you in. The distance will give you time to see if there's anyone in there or waiting to get in who gives you the creeps.

☐ Inside, stand next to the control panel. If you're in there with someone and something doesn't feel right, press the button and get off at a lower floor. Catch another elevator to get to your desired floor.

☐ Today's elevators have alarm systems that can't be shut off and are easy to access. I've been noticing that in many elevators the alarm is located at the bottom of the panel, about thigh level, easy to reach if you end up on the floor.

I know some of you like to take the stairs to burn those calories, but on the danger continuum, the elevator is way safer. It should be the only way you should travel between floors in a building. Think of a stairwell and ask the question, "Can anyone reach me in 30 seconds?" With the door closed and sometimes locked behind you, it is almost impossible for anyone to see or hear you unless they are in the stairwell themselves. When you are totally isolated like this and the bad guy is in there with you, he can take his time to do much more than just rob you. Police call this type of place the Secondary Location; NEVER allow yourself to be taken here. I'll talk more about this in Chapter 10.

☐ If you do use the stairs, have your cell phone with you. In many buildings, the door may lock as it closes behind you. You can use your cell phone to call someone in your office or hotel room to let you back in. Check to see if you get a signal here before you close the door behind you.

Your cell phone: an effective tool for self-defense

I'm going to digress here for a moment and talk about cell phones. Your cell phone is one of the most versatile and effective self-defense weapons you can carry. I strongly recommend getting one if you don't have one. It is useful for calling or texting for help, taking pictures of would-be bad guys, and can be a great tool for hitting someone harder, if it comes to that. There are calling plans available for as low as $10 per month.

Note that *any* charged-up cell phone, whether it has a service provider or not, can call 911. The only thing you need to remember is that if you do not have a service provider, you must tell the operator where you are located, as they cannot tell by the signal. I know most of you have some type of cell phone, but for those of you who don't, get a used one with its charger. Keep it charged up and carry it with you, even if you do not have a service provider. It could be better than any other weapon you might want to carry.

Cell phones can do so much more for you than just call or text people, as you'll see later in the book. In fact, I get so excited about the possibilities of your cell phone for safety, I'm going to bold the words **cell phone** from here on out, so you too will realize the power of this simple appliance.

One other thing, when you upgrade and get a new phone, please consider donating your old phone to the local women's shelter.

ATM

An ATM could be a marginal area, especially if it is located on a secluded back street or in an enclosed area. What is usual for people using the ATM? They go directly to the machine or stand a proper distance away if someone else is using it. They complete their transaction and go.

☐ Go inside the bank during business hours for financial transactions instead of using an ATM in the first place.

☐ If you must use an ATM, find one in a store or in a busy office building. The best places are where there are people walking by and where you can get help if you need it.

☐ Unless it's an emergency, use the ATM only during daylight hours.

☐ Look around the area before you use the machine. If you see people hanging around or the lights around an ATM are not working, find another machine to use.

☐ If someone is with you, have them watch behind you while you are focused with your transaction.

☐ If you are by yourself, stand with your body facing at an angle where you can see behind you, but still block the screen.

☐ After the transaction is finished, be sure to take your card out and put it back in your wallet along with your money before you turn away from the machine.

Other Marginal Areas

Think about areas that you might frequent that could be classified as marginal areas. Rooms where there is only one entrance/exit can be marginal areas if they are located away from general traffic areas. The usual thing is to go in to do whatever you need to do and go out. Public restrooms are a good example. In a busy mall or a freeway rest area during the day, the public restrooms are safer to use because there are more people in there. However, if they appear to be deserted, steer clear and find a better place to go.

☐ If you're in the mall, go into one of the department store restrooms instead of the ones situated in the mall itself. The mall restrooms can be rather creepy, often located down a long, bare hall. The nicest stores have little lounges attached where you can sit somewhere soft for a quiet minute of meditation.

☐ If you're on the road and need to use the restroom, stop at a fast food restaurant instead of using the highway rest area.

☐ Laundry rooms or Laundromats are also marginal areas. Pay attention to who comes in and out and leave when you see someone in there not doing what they are supposed to be doing.

☐ If you're at a party, even in your own house, any room away from the action is considered a marginal area. If you have to go to bed when your roommates are having people over, be sure to lock your door or use a door stop or door alarm.

☐ Don't go into a room alone with someone unless you are sure that they will respect your wishes. Make it a habit to note escape routes in a marginal area room, such as a door left cracked open, in case things go wrong. Stay where people can hear you if you need to call for help.

☐ It should go without saying that you need to stay away from high crime areas, places where people are abusing drugs, and places where people are planning or committing unlawful acts.

☐ If you do see criminal activity, in many cities you can call or send a text message reporting a crime to your local police department. Check to see if your town's police department offers a Crime Line text message address in addition to their call-in program. Your text or call should be considered anonymous and rewards of up to $1000 are given for accurate information. In Newport News, Virginia, for example, you can use your **cell phone** to text NoCrime@nngov.com with all suspicious activity.

PREVENTION AT HOME

Your home makes a fine shield to separate you from the bad guy. The goal is to reinforce this shield, making it difficult for him to get past the reinforcements and into your house or apartment. Remember, the bad guy wants to access your home easily, quickly, and quietly, without being seen. He may have been by to "case the joint." Do what you can to make him take extra time, create noise, or cause extra work for him to get in. He does not want to work very hard and will bypass your place to go somewhere else where it will be easier for him. Unfortunately, it is not enough to do just one of these things, as he's probably already planning to overcome one or two obstacles. You'll need to implement as many of these ideas as you can. Most are inexpensive and easy to do.

In your neighborhood

☐ Know your neighbors. Choose some that you trust. Good neighbors can keep an eye on your house when you're gone and can provide a safe haven where you and your family can go in case of emergency. Hope that the bad neighbors move away and are replaced by friendlier folk.

☐ Only put your number on the mailbox. If you have to use a name, use your first initial and last name. Put another fictitious name under yours if you're living alone.

☐ Keep your extra keys with your neighbors. The bad guy knows to look on the ledge or under the mat, and can spot a fake rock a mile away. The bad guys can find keys hidden within 40 feet of your door in places you imagine they will never look.

For people who come to the door

☐ Always keep your doors locked. If you live in a dorm or apartment building, do NOT prop the door open for friends to come in. Have them call you on their **cell phone** when they are approaching so you can unlock the door when they arrive.

☐ Make sure you can see who is at your front door. Install a view hole if you don't have one and use it. The wide angled ones are best. You can also get an inexpensive camera and connect it to your computer inside, so you can see who is there without going to the door.

☐ If you live in an apartment with a main entrance and see someone trying to get through your secure entrance without a key or code, keep them out. Speak up if you see someone "shadowing" another person in your building.

☐ If you don't know who is at the door, keep them out. Yell through the door to find out what they want. Only let people in if they have an appointment with you or if you have personally invited them. If they say they are from the cable or utility company, call that company to verify who that person is and if they are authorized to be there. If the utility company can't verify the person at your door, call 911.

☐ You can buy a rubber or metal door stop which will allow you to open the door partway, but can't be forced open.

☐ If you do have company-verified workers coming into your house, use your **cell phone** and www.mymobilewitness.com to document their presence there. This nifty service will allow you to email pictures from your **cell phone** to a secure online location only accessible by law enforcement officers. It's free and a great way to be able to get the bad guy in case there's trouble. Take the workers' picture before they get started with their job and let them know what it is for. Are you paranoid? No. Are you decreasing the chances that they will come back to rob or hurt you? You bet. Just that step alone might deter any criminal activity planned for later. See www.mymobilewitness.com for more information and how to set up your free account.

Inside your home

☐ If you're just moving in, change the locks. Install and use dead bolt locks, using a steel plate to reinforce the wood and replacing the short screws with extra long screws (2-3 inches). This makes it harder for the bad guy to kick the door in. Make sure your locks cannot be reached after breaking a nearby window. Two locks are better than one, and locks with a locking tongue are best. Ask your local home improvement store for their recommendations.

☐ Lock the windows closed on the first floor. Some windows have a setting where they can be locked in a specific position. Use window "stops" by putting a piece of wood in the top of older windows so the window cannot open more than a few inches. Another thing you can do is drill a hole in both frames when the window is closed and put a nail in that hole, which will lock it closed. You can also install inexpensive window alarms.

☐ Sliding glass doors can be installed incorrectly. If the sliding part is on the outside track, the bad guy can just lift the door panel out and walk right in. Get a track lock that will stop the door from sliding when you're not using it.

Phone Safety

☐ Bring your **cell phone** to bed with you. Keep your charger within reach of your nightstand so you won't forget, and charge it while you sleep. Imagine the situations when a charged-up **cell phone** on your nightstand in the middle of the night could come in handy.

☐ Make it look like there's more than one person who lives there if you live alone. Use a man's voice when recording your answering machine greeting.

☐ Have a generic message for your answering machine. Keep it the same whether you are home or away. Notes on your door for delivery people or friends will alert the bad guy that you're not home, and you don't want that.

☐ Just say no to telephone solicitors. My favorite line is "I don't participate in surveys. Please take me off of your call list." Interrupt their spiel if you have to.

Arm your yard

☐ Cut down high shrubbery near your house, especially near windows.

☐ Put one or more inside lights on a timer so you will have some lights on when you come home after dark. If you have more than one, make sure they turn on and off at different times.

☐ Light the outside of your house at night to make it easy for someone in your yard to be seen. Keep the front porch light on and install motion sensor lights for the sides and back of the house.

☐ Keep security lights too high for someone to reach and break. Low voltage lights and solar lighting save money and energy.

☐ Put lights in front of the garage so you can see the door before you raise it. Drive in so your headlights will light the way. Treat the doors of your garage with the same care as you treat the doors of your house, always keeping them closed and locked. Store and lock ladders and tools inside so the bad guy can't use them to get into your house.

☐ Lock your gates and have a fence. A picket fence is better than a solid fence which might shield the bad guy from view.

Keep your valuables safe

☐ Get a safe and use it to store your cash, jewelry, and financial or personal information. Using your social security number, checkbook, and credit card numbers, a bad guy can steal so much more than what you have in your house. Your passport alone can be worth up to $10,000 on the black market.

☐ Keep your big TV, computer, stereo, and other expensive electronics out of sight from the front windows. Etch your name on your electronics and use your camera to take a video of every room, describing each item out loud. Copy your video to a DVD, put it in your safe, and give a copy to a family member you trust. Label it "Grandpa's birthday" or something that you'll remember but won't alert the bad guy to an inventory of your belongings.

☐ Check out alarm companies for your home. Many charge an installation fee and then a monthly fee for their service. You can also use wireless alarms, doorstop alarms, or motion sensor alarms. If you do not have a whole-house alarm, buying a sticker advertising a generic alarm system might be a deterrent.

☐ The presence of a dog might signal too much trouble for the bad guy. If you do have a dog, know that your dog door can be accessed by a small child the bad guy might bring with him. If you don't have a dog, consider putting a large dog bowl on your porch.

If you suspect a break-in

☐ STAY OUT OF THE HOUSE if you notice something different about your house when you get home. You know what is normal.

If a door is left open, a window is broken, or something is missing, get out of your yard, go next door, and call 911. Let the police go in first in case someone is still there. That's their job. They are thrilled for the opportunity to catch a bad guy in action.

☐ If you are home and someone breaks in, call 911 as quietly as you can. Use your **cell phone** (the one charging next to your bed at night) if you can't get to a landline. Have a family plan to get everybody out of the house to a safer place. More about escape in Chapter 8.

☐ Have a local police officer come out to your home for a safety inspection. It's free, and they will look at your home from the perspective of the bad guy. They will point out which areas are vulnerable and alert you to blind spots where the bad guy can work and hide without the neighbors seeing him. They will provide a to-do list of ways that you can make your home safer.

☐ "Case the joint" yourself and see how easy (or hard) it is to break into.

IDENTITY THEFT

Your identity is one of the most valuable things you can protect. Thieves can go through your trash to get your discarded mail and documents. Armed with even a little personal information, they can trick you with phony emails or phone calls. With your social security number, credit card numbers, or any other personal information, they can ruin your credit and cost you a lot of money and heartache.

☐ Treat your social security number as if it were the Star of the East diamond. Only let others see it when they absolutely have to. Use some other number for your driver's license or any other documentation.

☐ Shred all documents containing personal information, including the pre-approved credit offers you get in the mail. Use a cross-cut shredder for best shredability.

☐ Just say no to telephone solicitors and surveys. Say, "I don't participate in surveys. Please take me off of your call list."

☐ Keep your PIN to yourself. If you receive a text requesting personal information from friends or family, call back to confirm and reply. If friends or family arrange a meeting by text, call back to confirm and reply.

☐ If someone calls and says they're from the bank or your credit card company, get their name and call them back using the published number of that company, not the number they gave you.

☐ Watch for "phishing." You all probably know by now that this is when you receive a scam email that looks like it's from your bank or some entity that you do business with asking you for your personal information. DO NOT click on any links from unsolicited email, including the request to "unsubscribe." Just ignore it and delete it. Call the bank or organization to see if the request is a valid one and if not, forward the email to their fraud department.

☐ Keep your computer safe from viruses by using a good firewall, anti-spyware, and anti-virus system. Open attachments only from people you know well. Visit www.OnGuardOnline.gov for more information.

☐ Vary your password for different accounts. Avoid the obvious personal information like birthdays and anniversaries, and names of kids or pets. One idea is to pick a song or phrase you like and use the first letters of each word. Incorporate numbers if you can. Example: IL2MIMI (I Like to Move It, Move It). Another idea is to replace regular letters with special characters, for example, $ for s, 3 for e, @ for a, etc. These things will make your passwords $tr0ng3r.

☐ Look for Https:// (with the s) in your address line to verify the address is a secure site. Check the icon at the bottom of your screen to verify it is a secure site as well.

☐ Make copies of your credit cards (front and back) and keep them in your safe.

☐ Compare your bank and credit card statements every month to transactions you've made. Call the credit card company if you have not received a bill for that month. The bad guy can steal your number and information, change the address to where the bills go, and charge up a storm with your card without you knowing it. To combat this, ask your credit organization to send your statements electronically.

☐ Go to www.AnnualCreditReport.com and get free credit reports once a year. Check them for irregularities.

☐ If your identity or credit cards are stolen, first file a police report, cancel your cards (see the number on the back of your copies), then call Equifax, Experian, and Trans Union (the three major credit reporting companies) with your name and social security number so they can issue a fraud alert.

☐ Some homeowner's insurance companies offer a rider for identity theft.

☐ Go to www.ftc.gov/bcp/edu/microsites/idtheft to reach the Federal Trade Commission's information on identity theft.

CAR SAFETY

Your car can be a great shield. When you are inside, you're surrounded by 4000 pounds of metal with the ability to go 0-50 in a few seconds. But it can also be part of a crime scene if you are not prepared. Prevent your vehicle from leaving you on the side of the road, keep it safe from the bad guys, and know how to use it to escape.

Before you leave the house

☐ Always keep your car maintained. At a minimum, check the oil and air in your tires frequently, especially before a trip. Learn how to do these checks if you don't know how, as well as how to add oil to the engine and air in your tires when they are low.

☐ Keep safety equipment in your car, especially in cold weather: a warm coat, gloves, a blanket in case you need to sit on the ground, water, an umbrella, jumper cables, flares, a small first-aid kit, a multi-tool with cutting capabilities, a flashlight, a pen, and a small notebook. Make sure your tire jack is in working order. Learn how to change a flat tire. It's really not that hard.

☐ Make a card for your wallet with emergency contacts and keep it near your drivers license. In addition, program your **cell phone** directory with ICE (In Case of Emergency) numbers. Put the letters ICE in front of the name of the person or people you would like emergency personnel to contact if you are in an accident. Emergency personnel can go to your phone and find ICE – John Smith or ICE – Mary Jones. If you've got more than one, you can program ICE1, ICE2, etc., for the order in which you would have the paramedics call family or friends to let them know you've been hurt. Plus, if you lose your **cell phone**, someone who finds it can go straight to the ICE numbers to reach you.

☐ Consider joining AAA or a similar program which offers emergency service when you have a problem.

Be a smart and courteous driver

☐ Fill up when your gas level gets under half of a tank. If you travel at night, keep the tank over one half full.

☐ Before you get going, lock the doors and keep them locked while you are driving. Many newer cars will do this automatically.

☐ Keep windows closed in traffic. Keep your purse or packages on the floor of the car or covered to avoid someone reaching in and grabbing your packages while you are stopped.

☐ Unplug and carry your GPS with you when you leave the car.

☐ In the car, limit distractions so you can pay attention to the driving job at hand. Make your **cell phone** calls and text your buddies after you pull over and stop the car in a safe place, and that includes hands-free calls. Put on your makeup and eat before you leave the house.

☐ Alternate your routine. Have a few different routes you can use to get to where you want to go.

☐ Only let people you know well ride with you. Drive by the hitchhikers and let the "friend of a friend" use their friend for a ride, not you.

☐ It's safe to be a courteous driver. Allow merging cars to get in front of you, and give the "thank-you wave" when someone lets you in front of them. If you make a mistake, gesture "I'm sorry." Assume that everybody is doing their best driving and give them a break.

☐ Give lots of space to any aggressive drivers. Move into another lane if they're tailgating and slow down if they cut in front of you. Stay out of any type of "road rage" situation. Pull over in a safe place and use your **cell phone** to report any problems in progress.

☐ At a traffic light, be sure to leave enough room between your car and the car in front of you so you can maneuver out of the lane if necessary. A simple rule is to be able to see the tires of the car in front of you when you stop.

If you have a problem on the road

☐ If someone bumps you, flip your hazard lights on and wave to them as you keep driving to the nearest public area to inspect the damage. DO NOT stop at the point of impact and get out to see what happened unless it is populated and well-lit.

☐ If your tire goes flat, drive to the nearest gas station or public place. I know it is not good for your tire or rim and you may incur the wrath of your husband or boyfriend. However, you only want to get out and change your tire (because now you know how to do it, right?) in a safe place. Use your **cell phone** to call for help if you need it.

☐ If you think someone is following you, drive around some corners. If you still see the car behind you, drive directly to the nearest well-lit public place, ideally a police or fire station. Blow your horn if you need to attract attention. DO NOT go home.

☐ If you see an unmarked car flashing its lights at you, put your flashers on, wave, and drive to a well-lit public place. Use your **cell phone** to call the police to let them know what is happening. Only open your door to an officer in uniform after you have verified that he was specifically sent there.

☐ Even after you have taken all of these precautions, if your car breaks down on a road with little traffic, pull over to the shoulder and call for help with your **cell phone**. Get the name of the officer who will be responding. If someone you don't know or didn't call comes up to help, roll your window down just a hair and tell them thanks, but the police are on their way. Make sure you only open the door for the uniformed officer who is responding to your call or to someone you know. There may be some situations where you will be safer if you leave the car and hide in the brush on the side of the road. Use your good judgment and let the police know where you are.

NO EXCEPTIONS

☐ Always turn the ignition off, lock the doors, and take your keys with you when you leave your car. NO EXCEPTIONS.

☐ Always take your kids with you when you leave your car. NO EXCEPTIONS.

☐ Always take your purse and other valuables with you. Store valuables in your trunk only if you do not have a trunk-opening latch inside the car. If the bad guy gets inside your car, he can get into your trunk.

☐ If you've had too much to drink or are fuzzy from medication, stay where you are. Call a taxi or let a well-known friend (not someone you just met) drive you home.

Your force field, the outermost layer of your personal protection plan, needs to be strong and redundant. However, when you use preventive measures for personal safety, it is easy to get complacent because you rarely know if any of the things you are doing have prevented a crime. If you are staying safe, it may be because of one thing you are doing or a combination of things. What you can do is to implement as many of these safety tips as you can, knowing that they have protected people who have used them in the past and they will very likely protect you as well.

Now, pick one or two of these safety options that you have not used before and put them in your Superpower Wallet. Implement them this week. Just add a couple for now. Reread this chapter next week and add a couple more safety options. Share these safety options with your friends. You are on your way to building the strongest force field that you can to shield you from intruders and attackers.

> *The ordinary acts we practice every day at home are of more importance to the soul than their simplicity might suggest.*
>
> – Thomas Moore

Chapter 4

Prevention While Traveling
The Power of Safe Journey

A traveler without observation is a bird without wings.

– Moslih Eddin Saadi

Whether traveling every week for your job or on a once-a-year vacation, there are different things to pay attention to when you're out of town. On one hand, you are extra-perceptive because you don't have the comfort of well-known places. Many people enjoy the travel experience more because they are forced to pay attention to details that they would usually miss in their home environment. Awareness is high. On the other hand, there will be situations that you have never dealt with before and you might be distracted by the details of just trying to get around. Just like when you're at home, the goal is to avoid crime by keeping the bad guy away from you and making it difficult for him to take your belongings or to hurt you.

Anyone who knows me knows that I have a passion for travel. I'm one of those crazy people who adores what many people consider the hassles of traveling; sitting on airplanes, sleeping in hotel beds, and eating out every night. I live for this stuff. Before I had my son, I worked in the travel industry for fifteen years and had the chance to travel all over the world. Then I married an engineer who just happens to be required to attend meetings in various European cities several times a year. I homeschool my son so that we can take advantage of these trips and go along with him. The result of this is that I have a boatload of frequent flyer points (which we use to go even farther away on vacation) and lots of experience using the tips below. So buckle up, put your own mask on before helping the person next to you, and let's take off with these travel safety tips.

Carry-on your luggage

One of the best safety travel tips you can implement is to travel with only carry-on baggage. Now, before you skip ahead to the next section, hear me out. It is so much easier to be aware of what is going on in a different city when you don't have to worry about how you're going to carry and protect something so big that you can only move it by rolling it. Most airlines allow you to carry on one piece of luggage (maximum dimensions 45 linear inches and 40 pounds) and one personal item (maximum dimensions 36 inches). Airlines will differ on these rules, so check with the airline you're using to verify carry-on allowances.

Although it seems that you need to bring more, you really can travel with two pairs of pants, up to five shirts, one sweater and light jacket, and one pair of shoes, in addition to the ones you are wearing. Roll clothes to conserve space. Throw in a couple of scarves to jazz things up. I can and do pack everything I need for any length of trip or destination, including cruises, in my carry-on luggage.

Pare down your cosmetics to what you actually use, and limit your liquids and gels to containers three ounces and under. Pack the liquids and gels together in a one-quart clear plastic zipper bag and keep it handy for security screening. You can find solid shampoo, conditioner, and body lotion (I like Lush brand) and powder makeup. Alternatively, it is fun to go to the grocery or drug store at your destination and pick up local varieties of toothpaste or shampoo. Leave the unused portion behind.

There are a multitude of benefits for carrying on your luggage. You will save money by avoiding checked luggage fees, you always have your luggage with you, and when you reach your destination, you won't have to worry about lifting a bag that is too heavy to carry very far. It is difficult for the airlines to lose your bags, you'll breeze straight past the people waiting for their luggage at baggage claim, and if you are connecting, it is easier to catch an earlier flight or be bumped for air credits or cash. Just try it one time. You'll never miss the stuff you thought you needed.

TRAVELING

✈ Make your reservations using a local travel agency or book directly with the airline. Online travel agencies are also fine to use, but they can have additional fees for changing your reservations. You should be able to easily get in touch with a representative of *the company who issued your airline ticket or documents* in case there is a problem. When you get your ticket from a travel agency, *they* are the ones that are issuing the ticket, not the airline. If the airline providing the service did not issue the ticket, they might not be able to help you at the airport if you have any problems with your trip or need to make any changes.

✈ If you're flying, make sure you have your seats assigned when you buy your ticket. If you're over 15 and are willing to follow emergency procedures, you can reserve a seat in the exit row to get a little more leg room. Consult www.seatguru.com, where you can look up seat configurations by flight number and determine which seats are best.

✈ Join the frequent flyer program of the airline you are flying, even if you don't plan to fly very often. Join the frequent traveler program of the hotel chain where you are staying and the car rental company you are using. You may get better service, the possibility of an upgrade, and credits for future travel.

✈ Get a passport if you don't have one and always keep your current passport up to date. You never know when a good travel opportunity will come up. It can take up to eight weeks to get a passport by mail without paying extra fees.

✈ If traveling internationally, check the State Department travel advisory for that country at www.travel.state.gov. They provide good advice as well as warnings.

BEFORE YOU LEAVE

✈ Stop the mail and paper or let your good neighbor pick them up for you. Have this neighbor put your trash out and keep an eye out for package deliveries. Mow the lawn before you leave.

✈ Put some timers on lights near the front windows of your house or apartment. If possible, put a timer on your television as well. Have them turn on and off at different times.

✈ Have one of your neighbors park their car in your driveway if you're driving your car to the airport.

✈ Leave a copy of your itinerary with a friend, the good neighbor, or family member.

✈ Leave your valuables at home. Wear jewelry that you can afford to lose or leave behind. Same goes for clothes. Bring only the credit cards you need for travel.

✈ Leave your metal nail file, Swiss army knife, metal wine opener, and lighter at home. See www.tsa.gov for other items that are not allowed for air travel.

✈ Bring a small flashlight.

✈ Make a copy of your passport, driver's license, insurance cards, and both sides of the credit cards you'll be traveling with and store them deep in your luggage, separately from your wallet. Use a black pen to cover up your name on the cards and the expiration dates on those copies, in case your luggage gets stolen.

✈ Using the ATM machine to get cash is often cheaper and easier than using traveler's checks.

✈ If you are traveling internationally or across the country, call your credit card company's fraud department and inform them of your plans. Some credit card companies may not allow you to charge in a far-away city because they assume that your card has been stolen.

✈ Use your **cell phone** or a camera to take a photo of your passport and any hotel confirmations or receipts you must present. Keep them on your camera for the duration of the trip.

✈ Bring your driver's license even if you are not planning to be driving. It is a great source of ID in addition to your passport, and is easier to carry and present in casual situations when your passport is not required.

✈ I also carry my AAA card, which is good for discounts at hotels and attractions.

✈ Bring a purse or bag that zips at the top. Your stuff won't fall out if you lay it down, and pickpockets will find it harder to access.

✈ Bring a money belt and use it under your clothes to foil pickpockets. Bring a small throw-away wallet and keep a couple of ones covered by a twenty inside it to use as a diversionary tactic in case you're confronted.

✈ Print out boarding passes in advance. Without any luggage to check in, you can go straight to security and bypass the line at the baggage check counter.

✈ Program the airline's and/or your travel agent's (if you used one) customer service number in your **cell phone**. Use the more exclusive number if you've signed up for their frequent flyer program, which should get you better service.

✈ Bring an empty water bottle and fill it up after you go through security. On the plane, I find I never get enough water when I want it.

➤ Since many flights within the United States do not offer food service at this time, bring some snack food or plan on getting something to eat at the airport to bring on the plane. You can purchase meals on the longer flights, but you won't even receive a bag of peanuts on most flights.

➤ Wear comfortable clothes that would be fitting in a casual public environment and shoes that are easy to remove. You want to blend in and not call undue attention to yourself.

AT THE AIRPORT

➤ If you did not print out your boarding passes at home and check in using the machines at the airport, use your booking number to access your record rather than your credit card number.

➤ Always allow yourself plenty of time for check-in. Get there two hours before your flight. Go straight through security with your carry-ons as soon as you get to the airport, or after checking your bags. Most airports now have restaurants, shops, and bars available after you pass through security, and it's the safest place to wait.

➤ Keep your boarding passes and ID accessible, but out of view.

➤ Make sure you can see your carry-ons as they go into the x-ray machine and that you retrieve them as soon as they come out. Put your luggage and laptop through first, shoes last.

➤ Keep careful watch on your computer, MP3 player, and any other electronics you will use at the airport. Record your laptop model and serial numbers before you go and always keep it out of sight when not in use.

➤ Keep your purse over your shoulder in front of you and your bags between or near your legs, in physical contact with you at all times.

➤ Do not take any packages offered to you by strangers. Do not offer to watch anybody else's luggage while you are waiting for the plane.

✈ Before you get on the plane, fill your water bottle.

✈ If there is a flight delay or cancellation, use your **cell phone** to call the airline or your travel agent for rebooking as you are standing in the long customer service line. You may be able to get your schedule changed by the time you reach the agent who will reissue your ticket.

✈ Get on the plane as early as you can and stow your carry-ons. With the current charges for checked luggage, more people are carrying on luggage and the overhead bins can get filled up quickly. If you signed up for the airline's frequent flyer program, you may be eligible for earlier boarding.

✈ Wear shoes that will accommodate swelling on the plane. It is best to leave them on for the entire flight. Absolutely leave them on during takeoff and landing. If I wear sandals on the plane, I bring a warm pair of socks in my carry-on.

✈ On the plane, eat light, sleep if you can, and drink lots of water. Move around every hour or so, even if only for some stretching in your seat.

✈ If you chat with your seatmate, be vague about where you're staying, especially if traveling alone. Just say no to any offers of transportation at your destination from people you've just met.

GETTING TO THE HOTEL

✈ Research your transportation options before you arrive. Know in general where your hotel is, how you will get there, and approximately how much it will cost. Check out www.ihatetaxis.com for ground transportation information.

✈ If you take a taxi, use only the licensed taxis from the taxi stand. If someone comes up to you and offers you a "special deal," pass them by. Verify the general rate for a direct route with the taxi driver. When in the taxi, ride in the back seat, make sure there are no other passengers than those in your party, and pay only after you have retrieved all of your belongings from the trunk. If the taxi driver creeps you out, have him let you out at a well-lighted, populated place. Use your **cell phone** to take a picture of the taxi driver or his license and send it to www.mymobilewitness.com.

➤ If renting a car, find out in advance what your existing insurance (home, auto, or credit card) will cover and what the procedure would be if you were in an accident. You can then make an informed decision whether or not to take the rental company's insurance.

➤ If you joined the rental car company's frequent renter program, go directly to their frequent renter lane. This will often result in a shorter wait for your car.

➤ When the courtesy shuttle drops you off at your car, make sure the area is well lit. If your car is parked in the dark, ask an employee to escort you there. Remember, the parking lot is a marginal area and you need to take the same precautions you would at home.

➤ Before driving off the rental company's lot, walk around the vehicle and inspect it for damages and scrapes. Make sure the tires have enough air and the lights and windshield wipers work and you know how to use them. Make sure the gas tank is full, unless stated otherwise in your contract. Report any damages or things that don't work to the rental agent and have them assign you a new car. Small damages that do not affect safety, like scratches, should be noted on the contract before you leave so you are not charged for those damages when you return the car.

➤ Know where you will be going from the rental car lot. Bring your GPS or consider renting one. At minimum, print maps and directions from www.mapquest.com or receive directions from Google maps texted to your **cell phone**.

➤ The same safety rules apply for driving a rental car in a different city as for your own car at home.

AT THE HOTEL

➤ Choose a hotel where you access your room from an inside corridor rather than from the outside parking lot. The walk from the reception area to your room is a marginal area. Notice what is usual and what is not. Get company if you see something unusual.

➤ If you joined the hotel chain's frequent stay program, go directly to the preferred traveler line upon check-in. It might result in a shorter wait to check in and a possible upgrade to a better room.

➤ Choose a room higher than the first floor (harder for the bad guy to access), but lower than the seventh floor (easier for you to escape).

➤ As you arrive at the hotel, have some small bills ready for tipping or small purchases.

➤ Make sure door and window locks work correctly. Use a rubber or metal stop or door alarm to secure your door.

➤ Lock your valuables, including your passport and extra money, in the hotel safe.

➤ Only open the door if you have requested a service. View visitors through the peep hole. Call the front desk if you have the least bit of doubt.

➤ In case the power goes out, use your charged-up **cell phone** as a weak light if you don't have a flashlight. You can also use your **cell phone** as a back up for the hotel's alarm clock.

➤ Put the "Do Not Disturb" sign on when you are in your room or if you go out for the evening.

➤ The hotel's fitness room is a marginal area. Make sure the door locks behind you. Most fitness areas are only accessible by the hotel guest's key cards. Use your good judgment if there's only one other guy in there.

➤ Keep your key card with you whenever you leave the room. Make sure it is not visible. Keep it away from your **cell phone** or any other electronics in your purse. The electronics may wipe out the information on your key card, making it unusable when you want to get into your room.

➤ Have acquaintances meet you in the lobby or restaurant, not your room.

➤ Carry a business card from the hotel with the local address and phone number on it. It's handy if you use the hotel's shuttle service to call for pick-up. You can show this card to a taxi driver if you can't pronounce the name of your hotel or street if you are in a foreign country. Also, there may be more than one Holiday Inn in that area.

➤ If you are a walker or jogger, check with the front desk or concierge for recommendations on safe places to go. They usually have a local map highlighting safe walking destinations or jogging trails.

➤ If you go out for a drink, be sure that you see where it came from and keep an eye on it. See Chapter 6 for more information regarding safety in a bar or party situation.

PUBLIC TRANSPORTATION

➤ If available, purchase your bus or train tickets in advance from the authorized person at the station. Beware of people trying to "help" you get bus or subway tickets from the machine.

➤ Have your tickets or exact change ready.

➤ When waiting for the bus or train, stand in a well-lit area around other people. If you get there earlier than other people, wait in a store nearby.

➤ People you don't know who engage you in conversation or ask you for "help" may be distracting you from another person who wants to take your luggage or purse. If you're standing in a train station or bus stop with your luggage, keep your bags between your feet with one eye on them if you have to talk to someone.

➤ Any bus, train, or subway can be a marginal area. Know what is usual. Choose a subway or train car with more people in it, rather than board an almost empty car. Sit up front by the driver. Watch who boards when you get on and get out. Wait for the next bus or train if you are not comfortable with the behavior of the people on it.

➤ Keep your purse over the opposite shoulder in front of you or under your coat with the top zipped up. Keep your important documents and funds in your money belt or wallet under your clothes.

➤ Hold your packages in your lap. They are harder to grab that way and you can move away fast if you need to.

➤ Keep your laptop and MP3 player zipped up and hidden in your purse or bag if you are on the bus or subway. Don't use them on public transportation. They can distract you and are an invitation for thieves.

➤ Stay awake or have a traveling partner watch out for you if you need to sleep on a longer train or bus ride. If you are in a compartment, lock it.

➤ Be among the first to exit the train or bus when it is at your stop. Pay attention in this marginal area.

➤ Watch out for people bumping into you or jostling you. I've known experienced travelers who've had their front pants pocket picked on a packed subway.

➤ When you step off the bus or come out of a subway station, instead of checking your map on the sidewalk, pop into a nearby store or restaurant to get your bearings.

➤ Walk along well-lit and populated routes, facing the traffic, in the middle of the sidewalk. The sidewalk can be a marginal area. If you notice something unusual on your side of the street, cross to the other side.

➤ Walk with head up, shoulders back, eyes alert. Look like you know where you are and where you're going, even if you may not.

➤ If you must use your MP3 player while walking or jogging (not recommended), use only one earbud, keeping one ear free for auditory danger clues. It's best, though, that you have both ears available to hear people or vehicles coming up behind you.

➤ If you must use your **cell phone** while walking (not recommended), keep your head up and scan the area around you. It's best to just find a place to stop and then make your call.

➤ Find out where the marginal neighborhoods are located and stay away from them.

Your force field of protection can be used anywhere. Travel should be exciting and fun, or at least with as few hassles as can be managed. It is no picnic when your purse gets stolen or you get hurt while you're traveling.

Close your eyes and imagine your Superpower Wallet. Imagine placing some of these ideas in there to use on your next trip. Think about them and try to create some of your own that might suit your particular situation. Exit this chapter carefully as we move on to the Power of Perception.

We live in a wonderful world that is full of beauty, charm, and adventure. There is no end to the adventures we can have if only we seek them with our eyes open.

-- Jawarharal Nehru

Chapter 5
Peripheral Perception
The Power of Practiced Awareness

*Live in each season as it passes; breathe the air, drink the drink,
taste the fruit, and resign yourself to the influences of each. Let
them be your only diet drink and botanical medicines.*

— Henry David Thoreau

Using Prevention and building up your force field will keep you
safe and hopefully will keep the bad guy far away from you. You
may never know if he decides to bypass your home because of the
locks and lights installed or leaves you alone on the bus because you
are sitting too close to the driver. You may never see him in these
situations and he may never see you as a possible victim.

There are situations, however, where you will be in the same place
as the bad guy and he will consider you as a possible victim. This is
where the second "P", or Perception, comes in. There are two types of
Perception. Peripheral Perception is when you are paying attention
to your surroundings – the world outside of you. Personal Perception
is when you are paying attention to the signals from your body – the
world inside you. Let's start with Peripheral Perception.

Peripheral Perception, or being aware of what is around you, will help you see the bad guy before he can get to you. We all know it is important to "be aware." But did you know that you can train yourself to perceive what's going on around you by *practicing* awareness? When you practice awareness, it is more difficult for the bad guy to get near you, and he needs to do just that in order to harm you. He's not going to rob you from across the parking lot or rape you from another room in the house. Practice being aware of what is normal and be alert for unusual activity. The bad guy will often choose to assault someone who is distracted and not paying attention over someone who sees him approach.

Practicing awareness vs. being aware

Practicing awareness is training yourself to keep your mind on what is happening around you at the present moment. What is going on right here and right now is all that matters. Your brain is tuning in to the reality of what is true and happening *now*, not making up stories about what could or could not happen. At any time, you are aware to some degree, but practicing awareness is a conscious decision you make to only pay attention to what is going on at that moment. With practice, you can train your subconscious to go directly to awareness mode in a stressful situation.

You may think that you are pretty "aware" and you are, to some degree. Every moment you are awake, you cycle through different degrees of awareness. Your awareness is probably most relaxed when you're at home in bed, just waking up, or going to sleep. You need to pay a little more attention when you are going down the stairs for breakfast, so your awareness increases. Awareness heightens when you are in your car, paying attention to the road, street signs, and other vehicles. Awareness increases further when you get into unfamiliar places. You are fully aware when you are working "in the zone" on a project or 100% focused on doing something you love to do. In that state, there is nothing else that matters except for what is going on in that present moment. As you move on to other activities, your awareness decreases. In a dangerous situation though, you want your awareness to be 100%.

Let's get real

So, how do you get to that 100% awareness more often? First, you have to face reality. Be aware that the bad guy exists in your world. Crime happens. You cannot afford to believe that it will never happen to you. You may be the only one around to protect yourself if you are alone. But remember, you have the right and the ability to keep yourself safe in a dangerous situation. Put up a good force field of protection and know your options if the bad guy gets inside. There are many women who have succeeded in avoiding assault, robbery, rape, and murder. That's reality.

However, awareness is NOT paranoia or fear. The *Random House Unabridged Dictionary* defines paranoia as "baseless or excessive suspicion of the motives of others." The key word here is "baseless." When you are aware, you are dealing with the reality of the present moment. The fear you might have when walking into a deserted parking lot is about an incident that *might* happen. It is not about what in reality is going on now. The reality is that a deserted parking lot means there's *nobody there. Nobody*, including the bad guy. If he's in the bushes or somewhere you can't see him, he is not a threat at this time. Remember, he needs to get close to you. If you're aware, you will notice him when he jumps out of the bushes or emerges from that recessed area near the elevators.

When you are worried or anxious, your mind is not dealing with the reality of now. Instead, it is in the future. Worry is putting your attention to a future that may or may not happen, but it is certainly not the reality of now. Put your energy and attention in the present moment. This is what you can control. This is where you can take action.

If the bad guy does suddenly appear and threaten you, you have a new reality and can access the Superpower Wallet of your subconscious to deal with him then. It is almost impossible for your brain to deal with the present and the future at the same time. Deal with the reality of the present and you will find that if you are calmly aware, there is no need to be afraid or paranoid.

Use your five senses

You can train yourself to use your senses of hearing, smell, taste, and touch, along with your sight to help you be more aware. Put aside your thoughts about every little thing and purposefully bring your full attention to what is going on around you right here and right now. Using your senses in the parking lot, you can hear the car engines and distinguish which cars are close and which are far away. You can hear the voices of a family walking to their van. You can smell the oil under the cars or the fresh air of the outdoors. You taste the cinnamon gum you just put in your mouth. You can see a clear way to get to your car and notice other cars and people in the area. You feel the keys in one hand and your packages in the other. Each of your senses provides information about what is real and happening now.

So, when you go into a marginal area, think, "Looks normal, check. Sounds normal, check. Smells normal, check." You may have to physically stop yourself as you enter and remind yourself what you need to do here. Place your attention and energy into what is actually happening, not what you are afraid might happen. Operating in the present is where you want to be, and you can train yourself to come into the here and now at any time.

Overcome distractions

It is easy to get distracted without thinking about it. When distracted, your awareness decreases. How many times have you found yourself driving down the freeway and forgot to take the exit because your mind was elsewhere? Many things can take you away from the present, from listening to the chatter in your head, to directing your attention to the inside of your purse, fumbling for your keys as you walk to your car in the parking lot. You can be walking down the street, thinking about things you need to do or talking on your **cell phone**, and walk right by where you wanted to go. I have gone from one room in the house to another to get something, and when I got there, I forgot what I was looking for. My mind was somewhere else. You can begin by being aware and have the best intentions, but sometimes your mind will wander away from the present.

Where did it go? Your mind was either replaying the past or speculating about the future. If your mind was somewhere else you were not where your body was. Think about it. If the bad guy is in the same place that your body is and he sees that your mind is elsewhere, he will take advantage of your mind's absence. He works fast and when you return to the present it may be too late. It is essential that you practice paying attention to when your mind has wandered elsewhere and practice techniques to bring it back.

Use your breath as a cue

Use your breath to help you practice awareness. Your breath is always happening right here, right now, and now, and now, and now. When you pay attention to the in and out of your breath, you are not in the past and not in the future. You're just here, now. Sit still, close your mouth, and just let your body breathe itself. Pay attention to the rhythm of your breathing and how the air feels going in and out of your nose. Did you notice how your mind forgot everything else but your breathing? By watching your breath, you can refocus on the present and retain that focus as you enter the parking lot or any marginal area.

Some people hold their breath when they're scared or stressed. Paying attention to your breathing will make it harder to do that. In *Mental Training for Peak Performance*, Steven Ungerleider, PhD, trainer for professional athletes, demonstrates how important it is to breathe when you're stressed out. Try this exercise. Take a breath and hold it for 30 seconds. Breathe out. Repeat three times. Do you feel the stress in your neck, chest, and shoulders? Nobody can perform their best with that kind of muscle constraint. Now take a couple of deep breaths, exhaling fully. Feel your muscles loosen up. When you breathe, you are more relaxed, and it's not just your muscles. You brain is also energized because you've brought oxygen to your blood.

Breathe right to increase awareness

So, is there a better way to breathe that will get the most oxygen into your body to provide energy and increase awareness? The Three-Part breath is well known to yoga practitioners and is a great breathing technique that will help you practice awareness. This type of breathing uses your entire body. Breathing this way, particularly when you are stressed, can help you be more focused on the present.

Let's back up the trolley for a moment. The way many of us normally breathe is to suck the belly in and tense the shoulders. This is shallow breathing. Shallow breathing actually makes you tired. When you get stressed, your breathing becomes faster and shallower. Fortunately, shallow breathing can be unlearned.

Use these instructions to learn and practice the Three-Part breath, a better way to breathe using your belly instead of your shoulders.

1. Sit up straight. Close your mouth and inhale through your nose, taking a couple of normal breaths. Put your hand on your belly.

2. Inhale deeply, filling your belly with your breath. You should feel it puff out like a balloon. As you breathe out, feel your belly contract as if it's pushing out all of the air that's in there. Use your abdominal muscles to force the air out.

3. Inhale again, and feel your belly expand out. But this time, when your belly is full of air, breathe in a bit more so that now your rib cage expands. Breathe out fully, first from your chest, then your belly.

4. Inhale again. Feel your belly expand out, then your rib cage, and now breathe in a little more so that your breath is filling the back of your throat, lifting your collarbones. Breathe out. Feel the energy moving in and out of your body.

5. The entire Three-Part Breath consists of breathing in with the air expanding your belly first, then your chest, then your collarbones. Breathing out throat first, then chest, then belly.

6. Continue smoothly for at least ten breaths.

Take a Three-Part breath, then a shallow breath. Feel the difference between the two different ways of breathing. Use the ring tone of your **cell phone** or some other environmental cue to remind you to breathe air into your belly. Do the Three-Part breath to music, or standing in line. Make it rhythmic. It's especially useful as you're getting ready for bed. When you find yourself breathing with your shoulders instead of your belly, practice awareness by changing how you breathe.

Better breathing is a great self-defense tool. It can remind you to bring your awareness to the present and give you energy, calmness, and focus. When you get into a marginal area, breathe. If you are nervous, breathe. Get into the habit of taking a few deep breaths every time you get into your car. Get into the habit every time you need to use the ATM or the elevator. Paying attention to your breath can help keep you safe.

Quiet the chatter

Probably the most distracting thing that can take you away from the present is that ongoing stream of chatter in your head. It's always talking, jabbering about what you should have done yesterday or what you need to do later. It might be telling you stories or complaining about something. Usually it is distracting you from yourself and the present moment. It's the reason you passed that freeway exit or forgot the bread when you went to the store.

The practice of meditation is one way to quiet that voice so you can pay better attention to what is going on in the present. In a dangerous situation, you want all of your attention focused on the business at hand, not the distracting voice in your head. Meditation is simply bypassing that voice in your head and practicing awareness. It can be as simple as taking a moment to quiet your chatter and pay attention to your surroundings. You can set aside a few minutes every day for meditation. There is absolutely no requirement to sit in any particular position or chant "om" unless you want to.

Here's how it works. Find a comfortable place to sit, close your eyes if you want, and quietly observe what is going on around you and inside of you. This is an active endeavor, so you should not find yourself falling asleep. Note your feelings, see them as separate from your self, and then let them go. Note the thoughts in your head. They're separate from your true self as well. Watch them float by like clouds passing overhead. They represent the past and the future. Let them go, because you are just interested in the present. Like any learned skill, if you practice awareness using meditation, you will find it easier to access when you need it.

An exercise in meditation

Try this exercise. Read this paragraph, then put the book down and do the exercise. Close your eyes. Is there chatter? Note it; don't try to suppress it. Watch it float out of consciousness. Beneath the chatter is your true self, watching the chatter float away. Instead of focusing on the chatter, focus externally on what you hear, what you smell, and what you feel on your skin. Are there any noises in the room or outside? Do you smell someone's perfume or food cooking? Is the air warm on your face or cold? What are your hands touching? Don't have an opinion or make up stories about these things, just notice them. Now open your eyes and see where you are. Notice things about the people around you. Notice details about the room. Try to do this once or twice a day, maybe first thing in the morning, before you go to bed at night, or when you need a break from what you're doing. That's Meditation 101.

What you want is a relaxed, yet alert, awareness. When you breathe deeply, you can notice your breath above other distractions. Use the breath to remind yourself to practice awareness. Breathe and pay attention using all of your senses in the various places you go. The next time you are walking outside, become aware of your breathing. When you do that, start noticing the details about where you are. What colors do you see? What are people wearing? Do you hear birds, footsteps? Does the air smell fresh? How does the ground feel under your feet as you walk? Blur your eyes a bit and notice what you can see peripherally. This, too, is meditation. You will be amazed at the details of life around you that you miss when you are listening to the chatter.

Perception is protection

Practicing awareness will help you increase your safety. When you are in your car, notice everything around you, to the exclusion of your chattering voice. When you enter a marginal area, use your breath to remind you to enhance your awareness to all of your senses. Pay attention to what is there. What is the reality of the moment? When you see something unusual, you can take measures to avoid it. Know that your awareness is a powerful deterrent for the bad guy.

Close your eyes. Imagine your Superpower Wallet. Open it up and put in breathing and awareness, your two new options to employ in a dangerous situation. Bring them out frequently and practice using them. Unlike the money we take out of our wallet and spend, the more we take these out and use them, the more valuable they will become. They will pay you back over and over again. Perception of your surroundings using breathing and awareness is an important tool for self-defense. Breathe in, breathe out. Now that you've got a handle on the world around you, let's check in with your inner world.

> For breath is life, and if you breathe
> you will live long on earth.
>
> –Sanskrit proverb

Chapter 6
Personal Perception
The Power of Intuition

*Intuition is a spiritual faculty and does not
explain, but simply points the way.*

--Florence Scovel Shinn

You've got your force field of Prevention in place and you are
breathing deeply, present in the moment with your Peripheral
Perception engaged. With these actions alone, you can avoid many
bad situations. So far, you have kept the bad guy on the outside of
your force field. Or have you?

"He doesn't look like a bad guy..."

We meet so many people in our day-to-day lives, and just about
every one of them are "good guys," people who respect us and have
no wish to harm us.

However, sometimes the bad guy can look and act like a good guy
in order to make you think that it is safe to let him get close to you.
Serial killer Ted Bundy raped and murdered at least 49 women.

Described as a "clean cut law student," he would wear a sling on his arm, making it look like he was disabled. He would ask a fellow female student to help him carry his books to his car, parked in an isolated area. When she leaned in to put the books in the back seat, he would ditch the sling, whip out a heavy iron bar and knock her out. He was then able to take her to a Secondary Location where he could rape and murder her. But to his victim, he was a good-looking guy who was nice to her and needed her help. There was nothing in his looks or demeanor that made her suspect trouble.

You probably know him

Although surprise stranger attacks get a lot of attention, most assaults on women are committed by someone they know or have been in contact with. It's a lot easier for the bad guy if you let him get close to you. He will pose as a nice guy, get close enough to talk to you, and test you to see if you will be an easy target. By seeing how you react to his guise and answer his questions, he will decide if he can get away with what he wants to do. This is called the "interview," and is the stage of the game where you need to bring in the next power, the power of your intuition.

What is intuition and how does it work?

Intuition is the "sixth sense" that you can add to your Perception practice. Practicing awareness involves using your five physical senses to look outside of yourself for danger. Intuition, or Personal Perception, is paying attention to your inner feelings, thoughts, and emotions. It's defined as "direct perception of truth, fact, etc., *independent of any reasoning process*" by the *Random House Dictionary* (italics mine). It's knowing that something is true without knowing why or how you know it. You can be sure about something, but you can't explain it logically. It comes as a feeling somewhere in your body or a thought that ignites your emotions. It can come by quick as a flash, or linger like a pain in your stomach. It could be your inner voice behind the chatter. We have all had messages from our intuition, sometimes only remembered afterward.

Why does intuition work? More than half of your ability to interpret the intent of another person is based on their body language. We instinctively know what another person's body language means through our accumulated knowledge and experience stored in the subconscious. Your subconscious can process more information faster than your conscious, thinking mind. Scientists report that the unconscious mind has the ability to process 11 million pieces of information per second, while the conscious, thinking mind can't handle more than about 40. Even though everything might look normal on the outside, your intuition can process the un-normal much more accurately than logical analysis. It can catch the tiny details that your conscious mind will overlook. Your intuition uses a combination of your senses, your experiences, and what you've learned in your lifetime to send you signals of danger when you need them.

Intuitive messages come to everybody and they come differently to each person. Using Personal Perception, you can determine how your intuition sends signals to you. Messages may come visually in images, instantaneously or while meditating, when you're in the shower, or when you wake up in the morning. They might come as something you hear inside your head, in the form of a voice or a thought, or maybe only one word. Physical hunches could show up as that sinking feeling in your stomach or in the tenseness of your shoulders. Some people receive their intuitive messages emotionally, feeling confusion as one type of signal or joy for another. Sometimes you get a hunch, and you just know. Some people want to make a joke about something that isn't that funny or just wonder about something they wouldn't normally pay attention to. Practicing awareness can help you determine how your intuition speaks to you.

Act immediately on intuitive signals

If you do receive an intuitive message warning you of danger, such as "this guy creeps me out" or "I wonder if he's an axe murderer," you need to act on it immediately. Psychological studies have shown that before you have the chance to think about a decision intellectually, there is a split second where you feel or sense that "hunch". If you wait too long, your "common sense" will take over. Don't get in the elevator with the one guy in it. Instead turn away, pretend that you forgot something, and then catch the next one. Go get some company to walk you to your car in the parking lot if something doesn't feel right. Go back to the party, if you're in a room alone with someone, when your intuition tells you to get out of there. Say "no thanks" to the guy that offers to help you when you didn't ask for it or need it. Put some distance between you and the guy who is getting too close, too fast. If you receive an intuitive message, don't blow it off. Act on it now.

How do you know it's your intuition speaking and not just the chatter in your head? An intuitive message *feels* right. You have a strong sense of what you need to do. You're excited if it tells you to move forward and feel a sense of dread if it tells you to hold back. One clue is to catch yourself arguing with your inner messenger. If you get that "gut feeling" signaling danger, yet try to justify to yourself, "I'm just being paranoid" or "He's such a nice guy," that's you trying to discredit your intuition. Stop arguing with it and act now. Decisions made by listening to your intuition will feel right, be right, and may save your life.

Barriers to intuitive signals

Intuition is available to you, but I'll bet you don't always use it. First, as a woman, you have received lots of training to ignore your intuitive signals. Your mother taught you that it is your duty to make everyone comfortable around you, despite what you feel. You learned that you should never offend anybody or hurt their feelings, even when you feel otherwise, or even when they act inappropriately. Perhaps as a child you were pressured to kiss or hug Uncle Adolf or Aunt Elvira when you didn't want to. You have been trained to ignore your inner messages in order to make other people feel comfortable.

Sometimes you just don't hear your intuition. Your mind is so cluttered with chatter that you are distracted to the point of deafness to your inner voice. Practicing awareness and meditation can help quiet the chatter. Other times you may hear it, but you disregard it. Maybe you've been having a few drinks and having too much "fun." Maybe it was just easier to go with that guy because he was "so nice." Maybe you don't want to be rude or called a bitch. Maybe your friends tell you what a great guy he is and you want to go along with them. It is important to realize when we push our intuition away.

It's OK to be rude

Here's a new rule. Give yourself permission to be rude to the bad guy. From now on, it's ok to be a "bitch" by saying "no." It's okay to step back or possibly hurt someone's feelings if you have the least bit of intuitive sense that they might hurt you. What a stranger thinks about you is not worth ruining your life. Take a minute to compare the risks: offending someone who you don't know and maybe embarrassing yourself OR saving your life and preventing a crime that will haunt you emotionally, physically, and psychologically for the rest of your life. Sexual assault victims live with the attack every day, and it affects not only their lives, but the lives of their families and friends. If you are practicing awareness, listening to your intuition, and there's a guy creeping you out, turn away from the elevator, or say "no thanks," and get back to the party. Get someone safe to accompany you if you're alone in a questionable marginal area.

I know that being rude is against so many things that you've been taught, but it is important to create a personal philosophy that no one will be allowed to violate your rights. You are allowed to protect your rights with "rude" behavior.

"I had a bad feeling..."

After attending meetings all day at a conference, I was walking down a city street in Los Angeles with my husband, George, and my friend Julie. As we passed by a gas station, a guy on crutches came toward us on the sidewalk from the gas station parking lot and asked if we could help him. George turned to him, ready to respond to his request. I kept on walking in front of him, hands up, saying "No, I'm sorry we can't help," and kept on going. The guy called "Hey, you don't even know what I needed help with!" George was astounded and said, "Wow! That was rude! What if he really needed help? He was on crutches. He couldn't have hurt us." I told him that I had a bad feeling and a voice inside me said to walk on.

After thinking about it for a few minutes, I realized that too many things were not right. In the parking lot of a busy gas station, why was he going to people on the street for help? We were wearing business clothes walking back from our meeting, definitely from out of town, perhaps easy targets. What if he had a friend behind some of the cars in the busy parking lot ready to grab our stuff? There were too many things that just did not seem right to me. I could have been wrong, but when he yelled at us that confirmed to me that I had made the right decision to keep walking. I did not feel bad about passing that guy by.

What if he is a good guy, maybe meaning well, just unaware of what the bad guys do? Say he really wants to help you with those groceries? A "no thanks" should set him straight. If he is a good guy, he'll give you your space and respect your wishes. If he's a bad guy, he may call you a bitch or some other names. That's your signal! You have made a good decision to keep him away. Anybody calling you names is not a good guy. Just let him go with the confirmation that you very possibly avoided major trouble.

When you do not listen to your intuition and cave in to your fear of hurting someone's feelings or insulting them, you leave yourself open for attack. The bad guy knows this and will take full advantage of it. Imagine this situation based on strategies the bad guy uses:

Laura was attending a conference out of town and staying at a hotel down the street from where her meetings were held. After a long day of meetings, she was heading back to her hotel, arms full of notebooks and her laptop bag slung over her shoulder. As she was waiting for a taxi, a nice-looking guy in a business suit came up to her and started politely chatting with her about the conference. He put his hand out and said,

"I'm Ethan." Laura juggled her notebooks, shook his hand, and replied, "I'm Laura. Nice to meet you." She had a bit of an uneasy feeling about him, but blew it off because he seemed like a nice guy.

The taxi pulled up and Laura told the taxi driver which hotel she was staying at. Ethan, right behind her, said, "What a coincidence, I'm staying there too. How about we share this cab, my treat." "Oh no, I can't accept that," Laura replied. "Sure you can," countered Ethan, "it's just a short way and it's the same cost whether it's one person or two. It doesn't make sense to take two cabs. Besides, you've got your hands full. You can pay the next time." "Well, ok, I guess you're right," Laura replied with a concerned look on her face as she got in, yet relieved a bit to let someone else handle this detail.

The conversation continued with Ethan saying that he was invited to the conference by his friend, Ben, who decided to go out that night with some people he just met from the conference. "I'm sure you've seen him, not too tall, and sort of balding, with a crooked nose. You know he got that nose from his boxing days. He's not boxing since that last knockout, though." Laura didn't remember seeing Ethan or Ben at any of the meetings, but it was a huge conference and there were many people there she didn't know.

When they arrived at the hotel, Laura got out as Ethan paid the fare. As they were going up the steps into the lobby, Laura dropped one of her notebooks. Ethan stooped to pick it up. "Here, let me carry those," he said. Immediately, she said, "Oh, that's nice of you to offer, but I've got it." He replied, "You've got a lot of books to carry. Come on, you're going to make me look bad in front of everybody." Not wanting him to feel bad, she agreed, and let him have her books.

They chatted some more as they walked toward the elevators. While holding her books on one arm, he reached his hand into one pocket, then another. "Shoot," he said, "I can't find my key! Looks like I'm going to have to wait in the lobby for Ben to come back and let me in." He looked at Laura. "I guess in the meantime, I can make sure you and your books get all the way up to your room." "Oh, no, that's ok," said Laura, really wanting to leave Ethan in the lobby. "I'm sure you'll want to stay here and wait for Ben; you'll miss him otherwise. I can take it from here." Ethan countered, "Ben told me he was going out with his friends, so I know he won't be back for awhile." He stepped back and looked at her. "Hey, you're not one of those women's-libbers who have to do everything themselves, are you? Look, we'll just go up to your floor and I'll let you have your books, I promise." "OK, OK," replied Laura, "It's just been a long day and I'm ready to go back to my room." "Well," Ethan replied, "it's just a short way. Let's get you to your room." He just wants to be helpful; Laura thought as she let him keep the books and pressed the button for the 20th floor.

In the elevator, Ethan stood right next to her, shoulders touching. Companionably, he struck up the conversation again. "I've been to so many of these conferences," he said. "I remember the one in Miami, where after the meetings, we all went to South Beach and really got wasted. Boy, those were the days!" By now Laura just wanted him to go away. They reached her floor and he held on to the books. "Come on, I'll walk you to your door. You won't be able to get your keys out when your arms are full of books! I promise I'll go back downstairs once you're in." Just wanting to get to her room and get rid of him, she sighed as she led him down the hall. As she got her key out, he took it from her, opened the door, and pushed her into the room. His promise turned out to be worthless.

Ethan, the "bad guy," used Laura's denial of her intuition to manipulate her into getting into her room. The types of subtle tactics he used were so close to what we might expect from people who don't hurt us, that they are hard to notice as danger signals.

In his book, *The Gift of Fear*, Gavin de Becker describes several survival signals which "red flag" a possible dangerous situation. I'll use Mr. de Becker's terms with my own interpretation of how they fit in Laura's story.

1. *"Forced Teaming"*

Ethan's first point of connection was to establish a commonality between him and Laura. He may or may not have been at the conference, (where were his notebooks?) but he wanted Laura to think that they had this in common. Every time he used the word "we," he was strengthening a bond that really didn't exist.

2. *"Charm and Niceness"*

How did Ethan get Laura to get past her initial creepy feeling? He was nice. He took advantage of the fact that we know nice people and they never hurt us. Hey, we are nice people ourselves (perhaps this is another point in common). However, acting nice and being a good guy are not the same. Niceness can be learned and used as a strategy to create trust. It is important to understand that a "nice guy" is not the same as a good guy. Your intuition is more credible than anyone's "niceness," which may very well be an act.

3. *"Too Many Details"*

We know the details of our friend's lives. After many experiences together and lots of long conversations, we know all kinds of details about the people we choose to spend time with. Someone you just met, a good guy, is going to be reticent about revealing too much information so soon in the relationship. In his conversation, Ethan included many details not asked for and not important to the conversation. His description of his roommate and his talk about his exploits in Miami were used to engage Laura, to get her mind off of what was actually going on. Too much unasked for information means that he's lying to you and trying to make himself sound credible. The good news is that if you're not sure and keep him talking, he'll usually contradict his made-up stories.

4. *"Typecasting"*

When someone says something that you believe isn't true, you speak up for yourself and deny it, right? When you deny an accusation to the bad guy, you are responding to him. He's got you talking to him and interacting with him emotionally, even on a small level such as this. When Ethan called Laura a "women's libber", she felt she had to deny this accusation, and it kept the conversation going long enough to get her to the elevator. The solution to this is to ignore the name-calling, offer no answer, and pretend you did not hear it.

5. ***"Loan Sharking"***

Anthropologists and sociologists agree that in just about any culture, there is an unwritten rule that, when one person has given another person something, the recipient must try to repay their benefactor in kind. Ethan offered to share the cab, picked up her dropped notebooks, and carried them up to her room without being asked. He was only using this "help" to get her to feel like she owed him something, even if it was just walking together in conversation. It's harder to ask someone to leave you alone right after they "gave" you something. If you're not comfortable with someone, you are not obligated to them no matter what they "give" you or how they help you, especially if it was not requested.

6. ***"The Unsolicited Promise"***

Anyone who makes unasked-for promises is trying to convince you of something that they sense you're not convinced about. This is not a guarantee of behavior or of character. Whenever you hear an unsolicited "I promise" from anyone, no matter what the situation, you should immediately question their motive. "I promise" is a red flag for highlighting your doubt and giving your intuition another chance to get a message to you.

7. ***"Discounting the Word 'NO'"***

This should be a warning sign for any type of relationship. If you are interacting with someone who is not respecting your wishes, it is very likely that you're going to get hurt, one way or another. Laura did not want help with the cab ride or with her books. She refused help and actually said no more than once. The person who does not take "no" for an answer is only interested in controlling you. When you let him override your refusals, you relinquish any power you have in the relationship. Any of you who have been around kids knows how this works. Kids will try to change your "no" to a "yes" or "maybe." The best defense is to say "no" clearly, no explanation required. No negotiation, no waffling. Say it loud if you have to. Parents and future parents out there, this is one of the best lessons you can teach your sons. When boys learn from an early age that no means no, the world will be a better place for women.

Here's another thing Ethan did that signaled his intent. Remember how close he got to Laura in the elevator? This was a test to see how physically close he could get to her without trouble. Any time someone touches you or gets close enough to touch you without your permission, they are too close. When Ethan sidled up to Laura in the elevator, he learned that he could get within her personal boundaries. Step away when someone gets too close. If they complain, tell them you need your personal space. Put your hands up, facing them, to make your point. Raise your voice if necessary.

Act on intuitive signals

Laura had a number of chances to avoid trouble. She could have caught that first impression of uneasiness and turned back into the conference hall to go to the ladies' room or find someone she knew. She could have said, "No," to Ethan as the cab pulled up and left without him. She could have refused his help with the books and hung onto them herself. She could have ignored his "women's libber" comment and left him in the lobby, or, maybe by that time, she could have asked a hotel employee to escort her up to her room. She could have even possibly left him in the elevator on her floor, watching as it went down.

Pay attention to your intuition. React immediately. If you miss the first or second signals, react on the third or fourth. Respond when you can. Don't blow your intuitive signals off. Make sure your decision making is not impaired because you're having too much "fun", messing around, or drinking. It is your responsibility to keep yourself safe. If you perceive little things that ignite your intuitive signals, you need to pay attention to what your senses are telling you and do something about it NOW.

Recognize intuitive messages with practice

You can practice being more aware of your intuition. If you remember it and the role that it plays in your safety, you will be less likely to deny it or ignore it. Think of times when your intuition has helped you. Through what sense did your intuition come? Make a note when you receive intuitive signals. Watch people in public, observing their non-verbal behavior, and guess what they're talking about or what they are feeling. Above all, keep an open mind and a non-judgmental attitude.

Now close your eyes and imagine your Superpower Wallet. Add intuition awareness, your Personal Perception, to its contents. Determine how you receive intuitive signals, watch for them, and act on them. Each day, when you practice being present, check in with your intuition. Remember how important it is, and that you will respect it, listen to it, and act on it when it sends you messages. Doesn't that feel right?

> *Presentiment is that long shadow on the lawn*
> *Indicative that suns go down;*
> *The notice to the startled grass*
> *That darkness is about to pass.*
>
> — Emily Dickinson

Chapter 7

Defending the Invisible Shield
The Power of Boundaries

Always act like you're wearing an invisible crown.

–Author Unknown

It is the intention of the bad guy to get within your invisible shield, confuse your intuition, and penetrate your boundaries to hurt you. Using Perception will help you recognize when you have a bad guy in your midst. If you recognize him as he is getting close or find him within your boundaries, it is not too late to get him out and keep him out. Let's consider where your boundaries are and how to defend them.

Define your physical boundaries

Whether you realize it or not, you already have physical and emotional boundaries in place. Your physical boundary defines how close someone can be near you before you are uncomfortable. It's that bubble surrounding you that defines "my space" from "your space." The size of that bubble can differ depending on the situation. In a large space like a hotel lobby, your boundary bubble will be larger than it will be in the elevator going up to your room or standing in line to get coffee. You will have a more relaxed boundary for a close family member or someone you're intimate with. Unconsciously, your intuition will let you know what is acceptable for you in different situations.

Experiment with a friend or family member to determine just where your physical boundaries are. Stand, facing each other, about five feet apart. As they are speaking to you, have them inch toward you, taking baby steps, until you feel the need to back up. Your boundary will be smaller for friends and family, but notice the feeling you get when even they get too close. Now, when you are out in public, pay attention to how close someone can get to you in various situations before you get that "gotta back up" feeling. Know how that signal feels in your body and use it to keep people at an appropriate distance. For most people, that is somewhere around five feet from you inside a populated space like an office lobby and ten feet from you in a marginal area. Only the good guys, the people you trust will not hurt you, should come within that five foot boundary, unless you're in a line, in a crowd, or some similar situation where it's acceptable to be closer to people.

The bad guy needs to get within your boundary bubble to hurt you. If someone you don't know or don't trust tries to get inside your established boundary, move out and away. For example, if a guy you don't know is coming toward you in a parking lot, move out of his route. He's a good guy if he keeps going past you, but if he continues toward you, you need to keep moving, keeping the cars as obstacles between you, until you reach a safe, well-lit, and populated area.

Send a message of strength with your stance

If you can't move away when the bad guy comes to the edge of your boundary, use your voice and body language to alert him that he needs to get out of your personal space. We'll talk about using your voice in the next chapter and concentrate on body language here. Just as your intuition sends messages to you about the bad guy, his intuition will receive messages about you from your body language.

The combination of how you stand, where you position your arms, and what you choose to look at can convey a very powerful message that will put him on alert.

There's a way to stand that will send the message that you have boundaries and are willing to defend them. Put this book down with the pages open so you can still read this and stand up. Shake your arms out. Now, roll your shoulders back. Notice that when you do that, your head comes up, your elbows go down, and your hands come in front of your body. Your hips are pushed forward a little bit and you are standing up straighter. Breathe deep from your belly and relax. Feel how your personal space has expanded out from your body.

Now, just for grins, let's try a posture that will be attractive to the bad guy. Keep standing, but roll your shoulders forward. Your head comes down, eyes go to the floor. How do you feel? What can you see? How big is your personal space now? When you walk around with slumped shoulders like this, you send the message that you might be depressed or have no energy. The bad guy is on the lookout for people with this type of posture and will single you out as an easy target if you walk around like this. Plus, as if you didn't need one more reason, sitting or standing slumped like this for long periods of time can lead to chronic back pain and the formation of that nasty dowager's hump.

So, your mother was right. Stand up straight! Roll your shoulders back again. Feel your chest open up and look around you. Keep your shoulders back even when you are sitting. In this posture, people can see that you are aware and confident. Use a cue to help you remember. How about every time you walk through a door, or even see a doorway, you do a shoulders check?

Once you're standing straight and relaxed, pay attention to your arms and hands. You will see later in the book that they make great weapons for defending yourself, but even standing still, arm and hand placement can convey confidence. In general, it is a good idea to keep your hands in front of you. Just make it a habit. Stay away from the "at ease" stance that you see in the military, where your hands are clasped behind your back. Think how vulnerable you are in this position. Your hands and arms are valuable weapons and you want them where you can use them at a moment's notice. Keep your hands out of your pockets for the same reason. When you are walking, release your arms and swing them freely and confidently.

Practice your Strong Stance

If someone is coming toward you and threatening your boundary, you need to send a "stop" signal. Drop or put down what you are carrying and roll your shoulders back. Step one foot back, so that your body is at an angle to the guy who is threatening you. Bend your elbows, keeping them close to your torso. Hold your hands open, about fifteen inches or so from your shoulders, fingers together, facing the guy. Look him in the eye. Breathe. This is body language for "back off, step back, I don't want any trouble." If there are any bystanders, it will be perfectly clear to them that you are in a confrontational situation. Try it where you're standing and see how you feel. You are strong, in control, and able to protect yourself. This is your Strong boundary-defending Stance.

You can take a variation of this stance with you wherever you go. Say you're walking down the street. Keep the main components of the stance, shoulders back, head up, arms and hands free. Practice awareness, naturally looking ahead and around the periphery. When someone walks toward you, approaching your boundary, meet their eyes for as long as it takes for them to see that you recognize them, and then move your gaze ahead. Eye contact is an important indicator of self-confidence. The fewer people on the street, the more important it is to visually acknowledge the person walking toward you. If you're in a marginal area and it sounds like someone might be behind you, turn around and give them a good look as well. Let them know you see them.

Define your emotional boundaries

In addition to your physical boundary, you also need to set your emotional boundary. This is your filter, allowing people in whose behavior is acceptable to you and keeping out people who are likely to hurt you. Your emotional boundary should be based on what is comfortable for you alone, and should not be based on anybody else's ideas. Only you can determine what your personal boundaries are. You have the right to decide who touches your body and how they do it. It is your responsibility to set these limits and enforce them for your safety and well-being.

Sometimes, in the heat of a new relationship, it is hard to separate the good guy from the bad guy. You deserve relationships with the good guys. Even better, incorporate these good guy qualities into your own life. Be like the people you want to attract. Use these qualities as a check list for any relationship you have, male or female.

The good guys are:

- Honest and up front with you in all aspects of their life

- Responsible for their actions and can admit when they make a mistake

- Communicating clearly and openly

- Respectfully listening when you speak and taking your opinions seriously, even if they disagree

- Willing to share their friends and family with you while allowing you to nurture and develop your own relationships

- Supportive of the work that you do and the goals you strive for

- Allowing you to be yourself and offering only constructive criticism

- Generally consistent with standards, moods, and personality

The bad guys are:

- Rude to anybody serving you when you go out

- Believing the rules don't include them

- Insensitive to others, putting their needs first and believing they are always right

- Weirdly quick about saying, "I love you" and want to spend an inordinate amount of time with you for a new relationship

- Trying to tell you what you are thinking and feeling, no matter what you say

- Talking down to you or calling you names if you don't agree with them

- Making "jokes" that are put-downs in public or in private

- Unfriendly to your friends or family and want you to avoid them

- Making everything your fault or someone else's fault when things don't go right

- Controlling with your money; they make your money "our" money without your permission

- Always asking you where you've been and who you've been with; they want to know what you're doing every minute of the day and possibly monitoring your phone calls

- Accusing you of being unfaithful with someone else

- Angry when you wear certain clothes

- Known to have a "temper," using hostile language, yelling, and breaking things in your house or things that have sentimental value to you

- Cycling between periods of meanness and periods of sweetness

- Using alcohol and drug abuse as an excuse for bad behavior

- Panicky if you want to break up, using threats and pleading to change your mind

💔 Hitting you on purpose

💔 Making you have sex when you don't want to or in ways you don't want to

People you hang out with should NEVER be emotionally, verbally, or physically abusive against you or anyone else. Red flag anybody who exhibits even one of these behaviors, although you'll probably find that where there's one, there will be more. If you see any of these signs in the person you are with, separate yourself from this person and get into counseling. You will probably notice that the severity of these characteristics will get progressively worse with the length of the relationship. Do not minimize it; you cannot control this situation. Staying with someone who exhibits bad guy behaviors is putting yourself, as well as any children in the household, in an unsafe situation.

Support is crucial

People who display these signs are not likely to change. Just about everyone who is married, or has been in a long term relationship, has gone into the relationship thinking their guy is a good person, but it would be so much better if he just changed one or two little things. Were you able to get him to change? Probably not. To get things to work, you probably changed your behavior to accommodate their "quirks." *It is impossible to change another person's behavior without their full participation.* If you are living with, or in a close relationship with, someone who exhibits bad guy behaviors, find someone safe to talk to. Get support from your family and friends. Call the National Domestic Violence Hotline at 1-800-799-SAFE. You do have options. There is hope, even though you may feel scared and alone.

Practice a strong emotional stance

Along with your physical stance, you can develop an emotional stance as well. Martha Beck, author and professional life coach (www.marthabeck.com), offers three principles to fight off the insults and "jokes" some people make with intent to humiliate.

First principle: create a strong emotional stance. You know how to stand so that your physical body will be better able to protect you. Now create a Strong Stance for your emotions. This means finding emotional balance within you, offering yourself forgiveness and compassion, and treating yourself like you treat your best friend or the person you love most. Be nice to yourself.

Principle two: Allow only the good guys within your emotional boundary. If you are hanging around someone who is hurting you, get away from them. You don't need to be around someone who is mean. Period.

Principle three: If the mean person you need to deal with is a neighbor, co-worker, or family member that you cannot escape from, there are some simple defenses that you can use. There are various situations where you can encounter meanness, and here are some ways to deal it.

Defenses against mean people

Sometimes people make remarks and you don't really know if they are intentionally cruel or just stupid. Usually they're kids or socially inept people that just say what they see. The other day my son remarked, "Mom, why do you have that one hair on your chin?" in front of a class I was teaching. So let's give them the benefit of the doubt and call them on it. When you hear a remark that strikes you as hurtful, turn to them and say, "Hey, that's not nice. Seriously. Stop it." If they didn't know they were being mean, you've educated them. If they were being mean, you've put them on notice that comments like that are not acceptable.

Say someone is outright accusing you of something. Your neighbor calls you an idiot because you voted Democrat (or Republican), your mother-in-law attacks your mothering skills by saying you should be sending your misbehaving kids to their room (or not), or your co-worker calls you a loser for some reason only they know. Don't fight it or argue with them about it. The martial art of hapkido has a principle of non-resistance, like air flowing over an airplane wing. Engage your strong emotional stance and just let it flow by and lift you up. Calmly reply, "I can understand how you feel that way. If I was you, I'd probably feel the same." You're not saying they're right, or agreeing with their assessment. You say quietly to yourself that they can say or believe whatever they want. It's a free country. You choose to believe your experience, they can believe theirs, and it's not going to trip you up. This makes for a strong emotional stance.

Sometimes the bad guy can belittle you or a friend in front of a group. When someone is being cruel, call him on it. Then go a little farther for the sake of the people in the group, who are undoubtedly very uncomfortable, but don't know what to say. Channel your inner Grandmother. "Now Phil," you can say in your best Grandmotherly voice, "that kind of petty meanness doesn't become you. Show us all that you can do better." This should diffuse the situation without causing a scene.

Close your eyes and imagine your Superpower Wallet. Open it up and now include your new boundary settings and the ways to defend them. During the day, if you find your shoulders slumping, sit or stand up a little straighter and roll your shoulders back. Breathe and smile. Review your relationships and spend more time with people who exhibit good guy behaviors. Think of how strong your physical and emotional boundaries are and remember that you now carry them with you everywhere you go.

It ain't what they call you; it's what you answer to.

– W.C. Fields

Chapter 8
Calling Out Sexual Assault
The Power of Voice

The moment we begin to fear the opinions of others and hesitate to tell the truth that is in us, and from motives of policy are silent when we should speak, the divine floods of light and life no longer flow into our souls.

— Elizabeth Cady Stanton

Using Perception will help you identify the guy you don't know well who is trying to manipulate you into a violent situation. Unfortunately, most sexual assaults are committed by people who you know and might have come to trust. You have an existing relationship with them and have let them inside your emotional boundary. They are considered "safe." Hopefully, you have now recognized the obvious bad guys and are keeping them outside of your boundary. But what about the ones who don't show their true colors right away, getting to know you and earning your trust with the intent of raping you?

The rapist you know

Many people assume that the average rapist is a stranger who comes out of nowhere and forces you to have sex with him. However, the most prevalent type of sexual assault is by *someone you know*. The Department of Justice 2007 statistics state that in seven out of ten assaults, the survivor knew her assailant. He could be a date, a co-worker, a neighbor, or a relative. You may have just met them and be on friendly terms, or have known them for many years, and your boundaries are relaxed around them.

Let's talk about rape and sexual assault. Law enforcement defines rape as sexual intercourse that is forced upon you. If you do not consent to sexual intercourse, or cannot consent because you are intoxicated or drugged, it is rape. It is rape whether it is vaginal or oral, and includes penetration by a foreign object. Sexual assault, also a crime, includes any kind of intentional touching of your genitals, groin area, buttocks or inner thigh, as well as your breasts, whether there is sexual penetration or not. The law covers female and male, homosexual or heterosexual.

It's not your fault when a rapist breaks the law

Here's the main thing to remember. Whatever happens, sexual assault or rape is *never* the fault of the woman who is attacked. Never. Never. Never. You have the right to say who touches your body and when. Anyone who touches your body without your consent is committing the crime of sexual assault. THEY are the bad guy. They are committing a crime that is not acceptable under any circumstances and you are not the cause of it.

Using Prevention and Perception, you can avoid many rape scenarios. Locking doors and keeping your senses alert in the parking lot will deter would-be rapists. Listening to your intuition and defining and strengthening your boundaries are also powerful deterrents. These work best against those three out of ten possible assailants who are strangers. But what about those people you know, the ones you want to get to know better?

Unfortunately, many assaults happen during or after a date. Date rape is the least reported type of assault because when it happens, the woman is often surprised because someone she let within her boundary violated her trust. Because of this, she is unsure if she is at fault and is embarrassed to let people know what happened. Here are some tips for avoiding rape and/or sexual assault on a date. You can also apply these tips to other intimate relationships, including those within your family.

Preventing date rape

✓ Do a little research on your prospective date. Talk to people. Google him. Try to determine that he has the same set of values as you do, particularly regarding sex. Sometimes, really good-looking and outwardly successful guys will have a sense of entitlement and believe that any woman that says no to them doesn't really mean it.

✓ Decide in advance if you are going to have sex. If you decide that this is not the night for sex, communicate it clearly to your date when the subject comes up.

✓ Keep your date in a public place if you don't know him well. Meet them at the restaurant or the movies, or if you're at a party, stay within view of the group. Avoid isolation in marginal areas such as his room during a party, your car or his car, your apartment, or secluded areas like a deserted beach or trail in the woods. Red flag: if you feel coerced in any way to go to these places, leave immediately.

✓ Bring your **cell phone**. Use www.mymobilewitness.com (see Chapter 2 for details) to take his picture and send it to a secure location. If he balks, tell him, "I promised my girlfriends I'd send them a picture of you!" A good guy should not have a problem with this. If there's a problem, go to the ladies' room and call a friend. Let someone know where you are in case your plans change.

✓ If you go out with your friends, go home with your friends. Make a pact that if one of the group looks like they're too drunk or impaired, another of you will stay with them and help them home. If you get split up and won't be going back to your room or apartment, use your **cell phone** to text or call your friends to let them know where you are. Send them a photo of who you're with and the front of the building where you end up. Send one to www. mymobilewitness.com as well.

✓ Watch for behaviors that might define your date as a "bad guy" or a "good guy". For instance, notice how he treats the servers at the bar or restaurant. (See Chapter 6)

✓ Stay sober and alert. A rapist will use alcohol as a tool to get you to lower your inhibitions and, therefore, your boundaries. I hate to be a wet blanket, but save the "buzz" for people who have proved trustworthy over time. If you have a drink, sip it slowly and make it last. Only drink while eating, or have a glass of water between drinks. Try a glass of sparkling water with a lime in it. It looks like a cocktail and may prevent people from asking you why you aren't drinking. Red flag: watch out for too much emphasis on how much you need to be drinking. If you're at a party where there are a lot of people drinking heavily, go home. Otherwise, you may end up with a bunch of really drunk people who might get overly aggressive and dangerous. End the date immediately if your date is drinking a lot or is taking drugs.

✓ Keep an eye on your drink at all times. Do not let it out of your sight. Take it to the bathroom if you have to and bring a napkin so you can safely put it on the floor if necessary. Pour your own drink or watch it as it is made. Open your own beer. If it tastes odd, spill it. Stay away from the big punch bowl and don't drink from a glass passed around to you. Watch your water or non-alcoholic drinks as well. Why? It is easy for the bad guy to slip a tasteless and odorless drug into your drink. These "date rape drugs" can cause loss of inhibition, loss of memory, drowsiness, and confusion. Some drugs cause physical illness such as nausea, seizures, lowered heart rate, and possible respiratory failure. They make it impossible for you to defend your boundaries. You will be incapable of resisting any advances and your memory will be wiped out. It is a federal offense for someone to give you these drugs without your knowledge or permission, with penalties running up to twenty years.

✓ If you feel ill or dizzy or confused, tell your friends (the ones you came with) and have them get you out of there and find someone who can help you. Make sure you mention to any medical personnel that you might have been drugged.

✓ If you see anyone receiving or administering date rape drugs, help the women who are there. Knock the drinks over, get everyone out of there who might have taken the drugs, and report this crime to the police.

✓ Just because your date buys you dinner or a drink does not mean that you are obligated to him in any way. Pay your own way to avoid any type of debt scenario. Watch for bad guy behaviors (see Chapter 6) and controlling tactics. If any appear, end the date. Trust your intuition and leave when you get that "got to get away from here" feeling.

✓ Keep a date you don't know well out of your apartment. He may plead, "One drink, then I'll go, *I promise*." Or "Can't I sleep on your couch?" Call him a cab if he can't make it home by himself.

✓ Be a clear communicator. "Yes" means yes and "no" means no. As things progress, every time he gets a little closer and doesn't hear "no," it's consent. Make sure your body language matches your spoken words. If you are making out and want to slow things down, stop what you're doing and state clearly what you want. Physically remove his hands from you, button up buttons and zip up zippers. Make your non-consent clear as soon as you want things to stop.

✓ Sometimes a guy will hear "no" and think it means "try harder." If any of you have been around kids you'll know what I mean. Probably every mom in America has given in after a few "no's" when your kids were pressuring you for something. Make it clear to your date that you are saying no and it means no. If he goes further, against your wishes, tell him that you will consider it sexual assault. You have the right to stop things at any time. However, if you're not clear how far you want to go and wait until just before intercourse, you may be making it harder for yourself to get out of this situation.

✓ If your date is a good guy, he will respect your wishes and not try to get you to do what you clearly don't want to do. A bad guy is going to try to manipulate you into giving in by using phrases like "I really love you," or "I'll just go a little way," or "if you really loved me…" You do not need to buy into this.

✓ Watch for things going bad. Communicate clearly and loudly what you want to happen. A clear stop is important. Don't worry about hurting his feelings or embarrassing yourself. It's a small price to pay to avoid the permanent trauma of sexual assault.

✓ Escape is your first priority if things go bad. Remain calm, breathe, and look for opportunities to get out of there.

✓ If he's not hearing "no," it's ok to lie to get out of there. Make up something that sounds like you are making the date better. "I have to go to the bathroom. I'll pee all over you and this bed if I can't go now. I'll be right back." Lie about getting more beer. Lie about feeling sick.

✓ If your date disregards your clear "no" and you can't escape, you can fight or you can submit. Chances of avoiding rape are better if you resist, but only you and your intuition will know what will keep you safe in any given scenario. Read Chapter 8 for more information on resisting.

✓ Any decision you make will be the right one. That you survived the situation is a victory and it is never, ever your fault.

What should you do if you are raped or you need to help a friend who was raped?

✓ Get to a safe place away from the assailant and call someone you trust for support.

✓ Get medical attention to detect sexually transmitted diseases and/or pregnancy. Do not change your clothes or take a shower; you'll need to save evidence. A hospital will have a "rape kit" exam, which will collect this evidence in case you decide to press charges. Without this, you will not have the evidence it takes to send the rapist to prison. Get a urine sample if you think drugs were involved. Pregnancy prevention treatment may be available.

✓ Document all details about the attacker and the assault. Write down every little, seemingly insignificant thing you can remember.

✓ Decide if you will report this to the police. Find someone who will help you understand your options.

✓ Seek counseling or call the National Sexual Assault Hotline: 1-800-656-HOPE. There are support groups in every community. It doesn't matter if it happened yesterday or many years ago.

✓ It's not your fault. Repeat this to yourself over and over. Believe it.

✓ If you have a friend who is raped, be there for her, listen to her story and believe her. Reassure her that it was not her fault no matter how it played out; don't be judgmental or blaming in any way. Be patient and let her seek help on her own timetable. If she goes public, stand behind her and get others to support her 100%.

The power of "NO"

One of the most effective weapons for avoiding assault is your voice. A good, loud "NO" can alert an attacker that you are not an easy target and can focus your energy for escape. It is good to practice saying "no," loudly and clearly.

Traditionally women have been conditioned to say yes, not argue, and keep the peace. You may not have a lot of practice saying no. When you really want to say no, you might get flustered and find it very hard to do. Not only is this a bad habit for your immediate safety, but, as you have more and more demands on your busy schedule, saying yes too often can cause you to become overworked and overstressed. When you say "yes" to someone else, too often it means saying "no" to yourself.

It will be easier to say no in a dangerous situation if you can practice saying no in everyday situations. How do you choose what to say no to? First, determine what is important in your life. Take an afternoon and prioritize the goals you want to accomplish. Say yes to the activities that support your most important goals. Make a separate list of things you want to stop doing. Consider cutting down on email, and only using your **cell phone** to make outgoing calls. When you get a request from someone who wants your time, let them know clearly that you have made a commitment to one of your priorities, such as spending more time with your family, and don't have the time to help them with their worthy cause. When you get used to saying no in everyday situations, it will be easier to say no in a more threatening scenario.

Commands are imperative

Defending your boundary requires clear communication without name calling or creating drama. Think about where your boundaries are with the different people you deal with. When they are crossed, it is your responsibility to let them know. Here's a simple formula you can use to alert people that they are crossing your boundary and making you feel unsafe. Point out what they are doing, state how you feel about it, and provide instructions for what needs to be done so that you are comfortable again. It goes:

"*When you do* action you don't like, example: put your hand on my leg, talk to me like that, drive so close to the car in front, pick your nose...

I feel how you feel about it, uncomfortable, hurt, unsafe, grossed out...

You need to state a command describing what they need to do to make you comfortable again, stop it, speak more respectfully, slow down until I can see the back tires of the car in front, do that somewhere else."

When you get into a boundary-defining situation, all of your instructions should be commands, not requests. I know you were taught to ask nicely and say please when you want something. You may even think you can achieve your goals with hinting around. However, these methods don't work with the bad guy. To get your message across, state what you want in a clear, concise manner. Repeat your commands and use the word "no" as often as necessary. Yeah, you might be called a bitch, but I like to think of that word as an acronym for Beautiful, Intelligent, Take Charge Heroine. This is your life, don't endanger it with unclear communication. If he's a good guy, he'll do what you tell him to do.

Yell, don't scream

If you set a strong boundary and the bad guy continues to cross it, you need to call attention to the situation using a louder voice. That voice needs to be a powerful yell, not a defenseless scream.

There is a big difference between yelling and screaming. A scream is high-pitched and comes from your throat. You'll hear it in the movies; probably the most famous scream is Janet Leigh getting stabbed to death in the movie "Psycho." Think of what is happening in movies where you hear this kind of shriek. Are the screaming women strong and actively defending themselves or are they weak and ready to succumb to the bad guy? Horror movie screaming will not get anyone's attention because we are used to hearing this kind of "fake" screaming when people are just teasing each other.

A yell comes from the center of your being. It should be low, deep and powerful, coming from the same place as your belly breath. Many Asian cultures believe that your chi, your life energy, comes from this point right below your belly button. When you yell, this energy is accessed, giving you extra strength and power to help you defend yourself. Plus, to someone on the street, it will attract attention because it sounds like the kind of trouble where someone genuinely needs help.

Let's practice! Stand up and get into your Strong Stance. Put your hands up, roll your shoulders back, and lean forward just a hair. Take a deep breath, letting your stomach expand as you fill your lungs. Tighten your abdominal muscles. This will allow you to control your exhalation from your diaphragm. Your yell will come from here. Now stick your tongue to the bottom of your mouth and be loud!

Since "no" is such a powerful word, let's start with that. Yell "NO!" Do it. "NO!" Concentrate on being comfortable with yelling. Try to make your yell deep and intense. Do you feel the power? You can practice yelling with any words that come to mind. I'm sure you have your own favorite word or phrase that you yell when you're angry. It's all good. Besides showing an attacker that you mean what you say, yelling releases tension, is good for your lungs, and energizes your being for escape in a dangerous situation.

Command performance

If there are people around, what you yell can alert others to help you. Make your yell a clear command, ideally providing direction to a single individual to help you. Yelling "Help!" is not clear enough, and usually people will ignore it because they might think it is just people teasing each other. If there is trouble in a crowd of people, it's a psychological phenomenon that when people don't see somebody else helping, they'll assume that no help is needed, no matter what is said, since nobody is responding to the call. If you yell "Fire!" people may or may not help you; some may even run the other way! Also, realize that when you yell "Fire" or "Help," you are in the mindset that you need someone else to save you. You have the power and ability to be your own protector and rescuer.

Yell "I'm hurt! Call 911!" and single out a particular person to help you. Most people have **cell phones** these days and it is easy and anonymous to call 911 and send help your way without getting personally involved. Studies have shown that an individual is more likely to help you if they are singled out in a crowd. Choose one person, identify them by some distinguishing feature, their clothing, for example, and give them a specific task. "You there, sir, in the green shirt, call 911, I'm hurt!"

Unfortunately, it is just as likely that you may be in a place where other people can't hear you because they are too far away. Maybe the music or some other noise is too loud. You need to make the bad guy stop in his tracks and let you go. Take a breath to remember to keep breathing and bring your awareness to now. Step back into Strong Stance and get angry about the situation. From the soul of your being, yell a command that you want him to stop what he is doing in no uncertain terms. Choose whatever word you like: NO, back off, get back, stop, and leave me alone are good places to start. If it's in your vocabulary and you want to throw in something stronger, feel free. Practice yelling "NO!" along with your favorite command, loud and clear for as long as it takes until you are safe.

Close your eyes and imagine your Superpower Wallet. Open it and put in your best yell, your best commands, and your best "NO! Get off me, leave me alone!" Know that they will be with you everywhere you go and you can use them anytime you need to. Once a week, open up your Wallet, bring them out, and yell in your house for practice, but don't scare the kids. In fact, teach them how to yell when they're in trouble, too!

That is slavery, not to speak one's thought.

– Euripides

Chapter 9
Explosive Techniques
The Power of Escape

*You are under the unfortunate delusion that simply
because you turn away from danger, you have no
courage. You're confusing courage with wisdom.*

– Source Unknown

Escaping from violence is the ultimate goal of successful self-defense. From the beginning of this book, the focus has been on keeping the bad guy away from you and you away from him. However, sometimes all the prevention in the world cannot keep you from a dangerous encounter. If you can't stop the bad guy from coming to you, then you need to do your best to get away from him.

There are two barriers to escape: not understanding what your body will involuntarily do in a violent encounter and the lack of a well thought out escape plan. You can overcome these barriers by making decisions and practicing escaping ahead of time while taking advantage of the stress reaction that accompanies an emergency situation.

Understand the stress reaction

Some self-defense classes are taught without regard to the psychological and physical stresses your body goes through when you are attacked and need to defend yourself or escape. I talked about this back in Chapter 2. When you feel threatened, your brain releases certain stress chemicals that bring about abrupt changes throughout your body. Think of a time when you were really scared, maybe when you had to stand up in front of a group or thought you lost your child in the supermarket. Remember that "deer in the headlights" feeling? Your mind went blank as you thought, "what do I do?" This was the result of the stress reaction.

In detail, here is what is happening to your body when you feel threatened. These stress chemicals, which include a powerful shot of adrenaline, are dumped into your system. Your heart rate increases. When it reaches 115 beats per minute, there is a reduction in the ability to perform fine motor skills, like phone dialing or signing your name, which affect the small muscles in your hands. As your heart rate increases to 145 beats per minute, complex motor skills, like golf or skiing, are reduced. At 170 beats per minute, perceptual changes occur, such as tunnel vision, auditory exclusion, and the feeling that everything around you is going in slow-motion. As your fine motor skills decrease (sewing not necessary for defense), your gross motor skills, like running or striking, get stronger as more blood is pumped to those large muscles.

Psychologically, your brain goes on auto-pilot for survival. Your subconscious mind takes over, which means your thinking mind can't develop strategies of what to do in real time. The subconscious mind will access only the simple directives that it has learned from repetitive physical and mental training. If there is nothing there because the situation is totally foreign to you, your body will freeze and your brain will go blank.

This stress reaction is involuntary. You can't stop it from happening. It's like when you put your hand on a hot stove. What happens? You touch that stove and your hand flies back to your body. Did you think about doing this? No! In fact, your other hand was probably in on it too, holding the burned hand after it came away from the stove. The stress reaction is as involuntary as your hand flying off that stove. However, if you know that it's coming, you can do some things that will make it work for you.

First, add information to your brain that will help you escape. This is where your Superpower Wallet comes in handy. Its contents, the knowledge and new habits you are learning, are for your subconscious brain to access in a violent situation. The prevention and awareness strategies that you are implementing, the recognition of your intuition, and the realignment of your boundaries are just a few chunks of information that your subconscious can recognize as helpful when a situation goes bad. Every time you access this information by practicing breathing, yelling, and being present, you strengthen the possibility that your brain will automatically use them in a dangerous situation.

Use your breath to calm your heart rate

It is the increase in heart rate which signals the release of the adrenaline cocktail that creates the changes in your brain. If you can keep your heart rate low when under stress, you can function better by inhibiting the stress reaction. Breath control can slow the increase of your heart rate.

There is a breathing technique taught to the military and police that is good in any super-stressful situation where you need to slow your heart rate down. You can use this in all kinds of situations where you're nervous or scared. It works whether you are physically or mentally threatened, so you can also use it before taking a test, giving a speech, or meeting the parents.

Let's try it right now. Take a deep belly breath in through your nose for four counts. Hold your breath here for four counts. Exhale through your mouth for four counts. Hold your breath again for four counts. Repeat these steps four times. This type of breathing will reduce your heartbeat and lower the likelihood that your perception will be impaired.

Develop muscle memory for your subconscious

Even if you slow your heart rate down by deep breathing, you will still probably have to deal with the loss of fine motor skills. Now, nobody's going to ask you to knit a sweater or play the piano, but there is one thing you will very possibly need to do with your fingers, and that's call 911. If an intruder is in your house and you can get to a phone, you've got to be able to remember and hit those numbers. Remembering to call may not be a problem, but dialing the phone might be. If you create the muscle memory for this important task, your subconscious will be able to implement it in an emergency situation.

Your **cell phone** might be different from your home or office phone, and you need to know exactly what buttons to push before hitting the numbers to get the call through. On my **cell phone** I dial 911, and then hit send. On my home phone, I hit talk, and then dial 911. Maybe in your office you have to dial 9 to get an outside line. Maybe you dial 311 for information more regularly than you have ever dialed 911. If all you remember is 911, and not what buttons you need to push in addition to that, you will not get through.

Lt. Colonel Dave Grossman, director of the Warrior Science Group, asserts that because you know that you will lose your fine motor skills when you are in a threatening situation, you should train your brain to hit the correct buttons automatically. Unplug your home phone and dial, "Talk 911," "Talk 911" (or whatever buttons you need to push to reach a 911 operator) in order, about 10 times. Have each member of your family (kids, too!) practice this. Do the same with your **cell phone**. Turn it off and dial, "911 send," "911 send" (or whatever your **cell phone** requires to get to a 911 operator). Practice this drill once a month. This may be the action that allows you to escape from a bad situation.

Family "Escape and Survive" Drill

Another way to arm your subconscious is to practice escaping. Implement a family plan for escaping from your home in case an intruder gets in. This also works as a fire drill. Sanford Strong, in *Strong on Defense*, suggests an "escape-and-survive" family drill. Instead of freezing, or running every which way when there is an emergency, you can create a plan that involves the whole family.

The first priority of the plan is to get the children out. It is easier for them to get away and get help, because an armed intruder will often go for the parents first. It is important to have an escape plan from each room in the house. You don't want to have only one perfect escape route because you might not be able to get to it. With the entire family, go into every room, no matter how small (walk-in closets included) and examine it for ways to escape. Explain that if there is an emergency, stay out of any rooms without windows unless those rooms are securely reinforced and impossible to enter from the outside. You can only escape from a room which has accessible windows. Guide the children to windows or doors that they can reach in case they end up by themselves in another room. In each room, make sure every family member chooses a door or a window for escape. Take your time and go through each and every room.

Run the drill once a month. Stress to the kids that it will be their job, a very important job, to go get help. The best way to help their family and specifically their parents is to escape first and get help. If they can do that, the parents can focus more on their own escape and not be worried about the kids. They will let someone know that their family is in trouble and send help.

If your house or apartment has more than one story to escape from, you need to make it easy and safe to get to the ground. Get a rope and knot it every four or five feet. Secure it to something heavy or unmovable in the room by the window, perhaps at the foot of the bed or to hooks screwed into the studs inside a closet. Keep it accessible under the bed or in the closet. A knotted rope is better than a rope ladder. Practice using this rope to escape, making sure there is something soft below in case of a fall.

Choose your good neighbor to be your safety neighbor. Have a couple of backups in case your first safety neighbor isn't home. Make sure the children know that when they get out of the house, they should be yelling as loud as they can. They can yell, "Call 911! Call 911!" or "I need Help! I need Help!" (You have practiced yelling with them, right?) When they get to the neighbors, keep yelling, ring the doorbell and bang on the door. If the neighbor has a home alarm, break the window to set it off. Instruct them to stay outside the neighbor's house. If no one comes to the door, then go to the second safety neighbor's house. When the child makes contact with someone who can help, have them stay with that person. Their job is then finished and they need to wait for the rest of the family. Put one of the older children in charge of the drill. Practicing this once a month with all family members present will provide the brain with instructions on what to do when you have to escape from your home.

Car Emergency Drill

You can also practice emergency drills for escaping with your car. Bring everyone out into the driveway and assign a seat for everyone in the car. Yell, "Emergency, get in the car!" as a signal to have everyone get into the car as fast as they can and get buckled up. Make sure that the driver puts the car in gear and pulls out of the driveway. When you're back in the driveway, advise the kids that because the bad guy will probably go for the parents first, it is their job to get out of the car as fast as possible and run for help. Now, when everyone is still inside the car, yell, "Emergency, get out, run!" Make sure that everyone can exit safely and don't forget to practice running for help. Use a stopwatch to time how fast everyone can get in and out.

Give up your stuff and run

Train your brain to know what to do by making important decisions in advance of a violent encounter. If the bad guy comes up to you and wants to take your belongings, decide now, in advance, to give them up and run. With this decision already made, your brain won't freeze as it struggles to determine what to defend in a real time situation. If the bad guy wants your purse, throw him your purse and run to a well-lit, populated place. If he wants your car, throw him the keys and run. If you carry money in a decoy wallet, give it up and run away from him toward safety. Give up your stuff and get out of there.

Giving up your stuff will help you determine if this guy is simply interested in robbing you or if he is using the robbery to get within your boundary. If the bad guy just wants to rob you, he should not be interested in you after he has your belongings. Stay safe by giving up your stuff and run away from there as fast as you can. Your adrenaline from the stress reaction and "flight" response will be helping you to run long and hard and fast to get to safety.

You can even give up your car to create a distraction which will buy time to help you escape. If the bad guy gets in your car when you are in it and attempts a carjacking, he wants to take you to a place where he can seriously hurt you without being seen or heard. You absolutely do not ever want to go there with him. Whether you are driving or not, grab the wheel and crash the car into something nearby, ideally when you're at a slow speed, then get out and run to safety. There's nothing like a car crash to draw people's attention, and the bad guy hates this.

Likewise, if you see someone in your driveway or garage who might be a bad guy, stay in your house (make sure your spouse stays in, too) and call 911. Let the police confront him; that's their job, not yours. The most important thing here is to remember that your life is more valuable than whatever is in your garage or your wallet.

Expect to get hurt and don't let it stop you

Another decision you will need to make is to accept that you will get hurt and it won't stop you from resisting and getting away. The bad guy knows you are afraid of getting hurt and that this fear can paralyze you from escaping. If you expect to get hurt, you are less susceptible to being controlled by the bad guy, and you want to stay in control. In a violent situation, it is easy to get overwhelmed with thoughts of avoiding injury, instead of thinking of how to avoid rape or murder. To survive and escape sexual assault or murder, you have to accept the fact that you will get injured. Face it, you will get hurt if you are assaulted and you will get hurt if you fight back. Remember the woman in the camping scenario? Like her, many assault survivors have risked getting hurt to survive. If you can accept the certainty of injury, you can focus exclusively on a successful escape.

In its brilliance, your body actually works with you to help you escape when injured. When you do get hurt, the stress reaction works to minimize injury to your body until you calm down and get help. In an emergency, blood will rush from your extremities to your heart to keep you moving. Your blood will clot, which means that if you sustain a knife wound or get shot, you will also lose much less blood. Normal flow will resume after you calm down and are in a safe place.

Most of you have never been seriously injured, knifed, or shot, but have survived cuts or burns, and for some of you, childbirth. You have survived pain and injury. So if you find yourself in a violent encounter with someone who has a weapon, be aware that a knife wound or gunshot wound is not necessarily going to kill you and you can live through the pain. In *Firearm Injury and Death from Crime, 1993-97*, the Department of Justice found that for every firearm-related homicide treated in the hospital, three and one-third were non-fatal. Not the best odds, I know, and in every situation there are variables that require you to use your best intuitive judgment. However, it is possible to survive a violent assault because a knife or gunshot wound is not necessarily fatal. Your body is made to sustain the pain until you are out of trouble and can get the help you need. Of course, every situation is different and if you decide to escape, make the decision that you will be OK with getting hurt.

Face your attacker

So, you're in the parking lot and the bad guy is closing in on your boundary. What do you do? Turn and look at him. Breathe. Bring your awareness to the present. Get into Strong Stance, taking a step back, standing up straight, and rolling your shoulders back. Put your hands up in front of you, palms facing him, not blocking your face. Even though you are in Strong Stance, your hands are up in "surrender position." You do not look like you are getting ready to fight or argue. Look him in the eye and tell him what he needs to do. State your commands in your regular voice. "Stop there. Back away. I don't want trouble." If he gets closer, repeat your commands, increasing the volume as you back up, keeping as much space as you can between you and him. If you're in the parking lot, use a car or your shopping cart as a barrier. The goal is to keep him out of your personal boundary space. Be loud enough so that nearby people can hear you and display defensive body language so they can see you. You want to keep him far enough away so you can run and escape from him if he tries to get closer.

Your arms are your shield

If the bad guy reaches into your personal space, you can use your forearms as a shield. Shield arms work in non-violent situations as well as violent situations. Say you met some guy at the bar and you're sitting there having a drink. He reaches to touch you. Bring your arms up (if they're not already up with elbows on the table), turn your shoulders at an angle to him, and make a waving motion that will brush his arm down and away from you. At the same time, communicate, "I'm not comfortable when you do that. Stop." Obviously, you don't want to yell here. If you get an argument from him, that's a sign of bad guy behavior (see Chapter 6) and you need to move away from him. Remember, you only want the good guys who respect your wishes within your personal space.

Stand up and try this with a partner. Have your partner reach for you and take a side-step so you are facing the outside of the arm that's reaching toward you. (If he can hug you, you are on the inside of his arm; we don't want that.) Wave his hand down and away so that both of his arms end up on his body, not yours. Communicate what you want them to do. If they don't comply, you are not getting the respect you deserve, so walk away.

Your shield arms are also useful in a more violent situation. If someone is trying to hit you, you can use your arms to protect your face. Stand in Strong Stance, step back, weight evenly balanced on your feet, put your arms up, hands open, fingers together. If you see a punch coming, step to the outside if you can, keep your hands up, and raise your forearms in front of your face to block the punch away from you. Your arms will get hit, but your face will be blocked.

If it looks like he's aiming for the side of your head, take the arm that's closest to where he will hit, and raise your elbow to point at the ceiling, keeping your hand close to your chest. Show him your armpit. Aim that armpit right at him. When you get comfortable with blocking punches to the side of your head, you can, at the same time, use your other hand to strike him in the face. I'll talk more about strikes in the next chapter.

It is important to stand up and practice these blocks to get them in your muscle memory. Get a partner and show them how to help you practice. Get into Strong Stance and instruct your partner to throw punches at you, one at a time, in slow motion. Successfully block each punch. They can speed it up once you get more practice. There is an old adage that says you have to practice slowly to go fast, and it certainly applies here. If your partner is one of those tough guys or gals who have to prove how fast they are or how you really don't know what you are doing, please educate them and slow them down. If they won't cooperate, find another partner, because they are NOT helping you.

Lower your center of gravity to escape

Somehow, the bad guy has gotten through your shield and is grabbing you by the wrist, wanting to pull you somewhere or try to hurt you. You want to make it as hard as possible for him to move you. React immediately. Yell, "NO!" As soon as he grabs you, put your free hand up to protect your face. One shield arm is better than none. Then, bend your knees a little to move your center of gravity down to your hips.

Here's where your beautiful backside comes in handy. You might hate what you think of as your big butt, but in a dangerous situation, the section of your body between your belly button and your crotch is the source of your power. Remember, our yells come from here. Think of your booty area as your own personal power plant. Nature has given you extra stuff there to protect the babies you are made to carry, so it is strong. Make it your anchor and use it to protect yourself.

If you lower your center of gravity to your hips and bend your knees in Strong Stance, you will be harder to pull. Try it. First, stand normally and have your partner try to pull you off balance. You stumbled, right? Now, take your shoulders back, step back with feet a little wider than hips' width apart, bend your knees a little bit, and imagine that you are rock solid from the waist down. Breathe. Think immovable as you physically and mentally lower your center of gravity to your booty and raise your hand up to protect your face. Can your partner pull you over so easily now? Probably not, unless he's the Hulk and you are Minnie Mouse. Your lowered center of gravity makes your stance stronger.

Your hand is the Star

However, you don't want to stay here, you want to escape and get your arm free from the grab. This is where your Star Hand comes into play. Standing here in Strong Stance, look at your hands. Palms are open and relaxed, ready for action. Take one hand and spread out your fingers, palm facing away from you, like you are admiring your new manicure or pretty ring. As you spread out your fingers, imagine rays of energy shooting out the tips like a star.

When your wrist is grabbed, step back and get into Stong Stance. Immediately spread out your fingers of the hand that is grabbed, feeling the energy shooting through them. Star Hand has been activated! Keep your other hand up to protect your face. Turn your Star Hand palm down and aim your thumb toward your chest. Then, remembering the power generating from your hips, step back and shoot your elbow toward the bad guy's elbow and jerk your thumb toward your chest. Yell a huge, "NO," when you do it. Your wrist should come free. Run like hell before the bad guy figures out what just happened.

If it doesn't work the first time, give the bad guy a kick in the knee or flick your fingernails in his face, which should distract him long enough to loosen his grip just for a second, and then break away with your Star Hand. Get a partner and try this. Practice in slow motion. You're grabbed, you yell, free hand goes up to protect face, step back, weight drops to hips, spread fingers out, palm down on grabbed hand, jerk thumb to chest as you step back, and run. Use your free hand to distract with a flick to the face or kick his knee if he doesn't loosen up at first.

When you practice, make sure you take a couple of run away steps when you've completed the breakaway. It's an integral part that should be included in your practice to build muscle memory. During a violent encounter, the brain's subconscious will go to the moves that you have practiced. You don't want to escape from the grip of the bad guy and still be standing there grinning at yourself for being so clever. Train your partner so they will allow you to break away from an easy grip at first, not the death grip, while you are trying to create some muscle memory for escape. Give them a fake kick in the knee or a flick in the face to loosen them up if you have to.

Escape is your greatest priority

If you have a plan and understand the stress reaction that will accompany the threat, you have a much greater chance of successful escape. Be prepared to give up your belongings. Accept that you will get hurt and it won't stop you from getting away. Practicing blocking punches and escaping a wrist grab will put more safety currency in your Superpower Wallet to be used in case of an emergency.

Close your eyes and imagine placing these options in your Superpower Wallet. If you review this material and practice escaping, dialing 911, blocking punches and breaking away from wrist grabs, your subconscious will have something to turn to when you get in a dangerous situation. The chance of your successful escape increases the more you practice and review. Every time that you physically repeat these moves, you build the muscle memory that your subconscious will access to get you safe. When you add these escapes to your awareness, breathing, intuition, and strong boundaries, you are building a huge arsenal of Superpowers.

Make your feet your friend.

– J.M. Barrie

Chapter 10

Deploying Your Personal Weapons
The Power of the Angry Attack

There is a kind of physical pleasure in resisting an iniquitous power.

– Germaine de Stael

Even after all the precautions you have taken, you may still end up in a situation where you can't escape with a simple breakaway.

If someone is in your boundary, even after you have given them ample warning to get to a more acceptable distance and given up the stuff they wanted, you've got to assume that they intend to hurt you. Any guy who is inside your boundary and is trying to restrain you is *not* a guy you want to give the benefit of the doubt to. He may be threatening you with or without a weapon, holding you down, or intending to hit you with something. He has broken the rules and now you have to assume that his plan is to harm you. You cannot treat him like a rational human being anymore, because he isn't. He is alien, like nobody you have ever met. You must assume that he doesn't care whether you live or die, as long as he gets to do what he wants.

Get mad to generate power

So how do you react to someone breaking the rules like this?
You have to get angry; really, really, pissed! This guy is a criminal
who, if he succeeds, will change your life *and the lives of people you
love* forever. The physical assault itself is only the beginning of
the trauma of rape. Survivors of assault are often troubled by a
range of symptoms, including unexplained body pain, nightmares
and sleeplessness, fear, anxiety, major depression, and inability
to function socially. What's worse is that it's not just you who
suffers. A violent assault affects not only your life, but the lives of
everybody who cares about you. It's as if you and each of the people
you care about are assaulted over and over again. So, when the bad
guy comes within your boundary, GET MAD, if not for yourself then
for what that assault could do to your family. This guy does not
belong on the streets. He will hurt you, someone you love, or some
other woman who does not deserve it. You could be in a position to
stop him and have the right and ability to defend yourself.

Resist or submit?

When you are in a situation where the bad guy is threatening you
within your boundaries, you have two choices: resist or submit.
I can't tell you which one is right for whatever situation you may
find yourself, because there are so many variables. This is where
you need to listen to your intuition and use the knowledge you
have to make the best decision possible. Resist or submit, there is
no judgment either way. Understand though, that as long as you
submit, you are placing yourself under the bad guy's control. There
may be some situations where you will need to submit, during the
entire assault or maybe just for a little while until you can escape
more easily, if it will save your life. Only you are the best judge of
what is the right thing to do.

Regarding resisting, studies have shown that when a woman resists
sexual assault, she is more likely to escape. Dr. Judith Herman
published studies on this topic in her book *Trauma and Recovery*.
She found that women who resisted and fought back were more

likely to avoid sexual assault than women who chose to submit, whether or not a weapon was present. Resisting would not "make things worse." She also found that strategies such as pleading, crying, or trying to reason with the attacker were ineffective and sometimes counterproductive. Women who resisted were also less likely to suffer from post-attack distress.

The bad guy is committed to hurting you and when you submit, he will carry out his plan, no matter what you say to try to dissuade him. He has willfully blown off all of your clear signals to get away. So what do you do? If you *react immediately, resist loudly and explosively, with determined angry intention to get away from him, chances are better that you will escape the assault.*

The bad guy will lie to you

One reason that a woman might not resist is that she believes what the rapist is telling her. He's going to say that if you're quiet and go along with him, he won't hurt you. Think about it. He is *promising* not to hurt you. Not getting hurt is what you really want, right? It's tempting to think that there is an option that does not require action on your part to get out of this situation. You want to believe him, but it's a false option; *he's lying to you.* He is threatening you with getting hurt because he knows that most women are seriously afraid of getting hurt. He knows that somewhere inside you want to believe him and he is using that against you.

When you hear the bad guy giving you instructions, he is in fact telling you what to do to make it easier for him to hurt you. He is lying about not hurting you, because he knows there's a pretty good chance that you will believe him. You may want to, but DO NOT believe him. He's not some misguided person that needs your empathy and attention. He is a liar, a rapist, and possibly a murderer. If there is any chance that he might deprive your family of their mother, daughter, or spouse, you need to understand that he is lying. When you hear him giving you directions in order to make it easier for him, you must think about doing the opposite. Your first contact with him is at Crime Scene Number One. If you resist and make noise, aiming to get to safety, there is less chance he will take you to Crime Scene Number Two.

Avoid the Secondary Location at all costs

You should always resist when he wants to take you to a Secondary Location, or, as the police call it, Crime Scene Number Two. It is usually inconvenient to impossible for him to commit a crime at Crime Scene Number One, your first contact with him. If he can get you to a place where no one can see him or hear you, he, and possibly some of his friends, will be able to carry out the assault, rape and/or murder he has planned. Once you are moved to Crime Scene Number Two, know that he will certainly have handcuffs, duct tape, a belt, or some other restraint to bind you, making your ability to fight back and/or escape almost impossible. At the Secondary Location, there are no people to help who can see you or hear you. He can do whatever he wants to you, and your chances of survival plummet if you let him take you there. This is why you must resist immediately, explosively, and loudly, if it looks like he can transport you away from Crime Scene Number One.

Plan in advance how to react if you are being grabbed or hit and can't run away. The bad guy's plan is to target a person who he can easily get to a Secondary Location. Make yourself the hardest target you can be. If you get really angry and continue to yell, step into Strong Stance, and sink your weight into your hips, it will make it extremely difficult for him to take you anywhere. If you're in your car, remember the attention-attracting escape strategy of crashing it into something while you're still in a populated area, or anywhere, for that matter. When you react immediately, yelling loudly and clearly, you make it harder for the bad guy to hurt you.

You are so striking!

If you're not in a place where you can draw attention to your situation, then your goal is to disable the guy so that you can get away. That means hit him hard over and over until you can escape.

To be effective, you have to overcome your cultural training. Most women have been taught never to hit, and if you're somebody's mom or babysitter, you probably have told the children you're in charge of not to hit. Many boys grow up wrestling and tussling; they know how to react to physical contact. It's in their muscle memory from all that practice. Not only are you missing that muscle memory, you have been socially conditioned that girls don't fight. Have you ever spent time imagining hitting anyone as hard as you can? Probably not.

When I talk about striking the bad guy, know that your prime objective is escape. This is not a fight. You need to get the bad guy away from you. He won't respond to any reasonable method. You can't talk him out of it. At this point, you are only going to escape if you disable him by striking him in his vulnerable areas. If his vision is impaired because you broke his nose with your elbow or stuck three fingers in his eye, chances are better that he will be concerned with his own injuries long enough for you to escape.

Take a self-defense course for more practice

It is beyond the scope of this book to teach you how to escape from every hold and to guarantee that you can physically fight your way out. There are many good self-defense classes where you can get hands-on experience. One really great short-term option is the R.A.D. (Rape Aggression Defense) self-defense training. These physically active classes are exclusively for women and offered by many local police stations and college campuses. The three-to-five class curriculum ends with a session where a guy covered in padding is available for you to strike as hard as you can with your newly acquired moves. Plus, once you attend one session, you are welcome to return and retake the class for free at any other time. See www. rad-systems.com to locate a class near you. Classes like these are great for learning escapes and strikes to add to your safety Wallet. It's a small investment with a huge payoff. Every woman (and her teenage daughter) should take this class.

For a greater commitment, the best on-going self-defense training course that I know is with the International Combat Hapkido Federation (ICHF). Yeah, I know it sounds like a bunch of G.I. Joes fighting each other, but its creator, Grandmaster Pellegrini, has taken the Korean martial art of hapkido and brought it up to date to suit today's practical self-defense situations. I think it's especially good for women because it relies on joint manipulation to disable the attacker. It doesn't take that much strength to bend someone's wrist the wrong way. Most guys who work out, no matter what their size, are not training their knees or fingers to bend backwards. With this kind of training and practice, you can learn to get the bad guy to the ground by twisting his wrist the wrong way or disabling his knee. The Combat Hapkido system also teaches you to strike vulnerable, vital points of the human anatomy for maximum results. These strikes do not require strong physical force, just speed and accurate connection to the targets. They will generate great pain, loss of motor function, brain overload, and incapacitation.

Most of the ICHF centers are run by men and you will find more men than women in the classes. However, women are welcome and treated respectfully. They have a children's program, too. The presence of so many men is a good thing, because you almost always have a good guy who is bigger than you to practice on which makes the training very realistic. One caveat: because you can't learn a wrist lock unless you've experienced it yourself, make sure you are ready for the experience of having your wrists bent back and being twisted to the ground yourself in this kind of training. It's not for everyone, but it is a very effective, practical way to learn and practice self-defense tactics. See www.dsihq.com for more details.

When you take any self-defense course, you have the opportunity to energetically build the muscle memory that your brain will turn to in a stressful situation. However, there is no self-defense course that will guarantee your safety. There's no one move, or set of moves, that will work on every person, at every time. Every situation is different, every person is different, and whatever you do will be the best that you can do in that situation. However, your chances of survival will increase as you learn and train, have a plan to review what you learned, and practice it on a regular basis.

Your body is an arsenal of weapons

We have already determined that to successfully escape, you may need to use physical force against your attacker. Here's the good news: you have some truly strong places on your body that can really hurt someone. More good news: the bad guy has some distinctly vulnerable places that he cannot strengthen no matter how hard he works out. When you attack these vulnerable areas using the strong parts of your body, you can cause enough pain and incapacitation to escape.

The most effective parts on your body that you can use as weapons are bony and hard: your fingers, hands, elbows, knees, and feet. These are weapons that can be powered using gross motor skills, which, if you recall, will be enhanced during the stress reaction. These weapons are with you all the time, they don't need to be sharpened or loaded, and they are easy to control. Most importantly, they can cause enough damage to disable an attacker.

Each of these weapons can be used in various ways.

✳ **Fingers** – It is most effective to use all of your fingers bunched together as a spear and aim for something soft, like an eyeball. One or two fingers are ok, but many fingers working with each other are stronger. Hold your fingers together and bend each of them slightly in. Bending your fingers in a bit will keep them from breaking backwards if they hit something hard by mistake.

✳ **Hands** – You can use your hands at least three different ways: make a fist and use it as a hammer, turn your fist around and smack your attacker with your knuckles, or open your hand and use the heel of your palm to strike. Some courses teach punching, and perhaps some of you have practiced punching the air in your kickboxing class. Personally, I'm not a big fan of women punching bad guys for self-defense. Here's my rule: if you don't have practice punching solid targets, don't punch the bad guy. It is hard on your wrist and it hurts. Instead, use the palm heel strike. It is much more powerful. Your hand is already open in your Strong Stance, and when you strike with the base of your palm, there are no little bones to get broken or hurt. When you use your palm, your wrist is aligned with your entire arm and you've got the power of your whole body behind it. Use your hips to pivot as you strike.

✸ **Elbows** – Your elbow across a bad guy's face can cut his skin. From Strong Stance, you can bring your elbow straight up in front of you to his face or turn your palm down and bring your elbow across the side of his face or throat. Keep your Star Hand open and energized as you did in the breakaway. Imagine the power flowing from your hips, up your arm, and out of your extended fingers in this devastating move.

✸ **Knees** – Your legs are the most powerful limbs on your body. Use the power generated from your hips for a full force strike. You can knee anything that comes close to your legs. A bad guy's head, if he bends over, is a great target. Make sure you grab the back of whatever you're going to strike to keep it in place. The groin is another great target, but if you can't reach it, you can also aim for the inside of the leg above the knee, on the outside of the thigh, or right above the knee joint. A knee strike on any of these points has a good chance of making his legs buckle.

✸ **Feet** – Keep your feet about knee height when you kick. In fact, the knee is a fantastic target for a powerful, fast kick. Curl your toes back and use the ball of your foot if you're kicking straight on, or turn your hips and kick out sideways, aiming the outside edge of your foot and heel at the target. Stomping straight down the shin to the foot works especially well with heels.

A good strike is fast and uses all the force you can muster right from where you are standing. Don't wind-up before you strike; this will alert him to your plan. You will have plenty of power from your Strong Stance because you are unbelievably angry and have a powerful intention to escape. Plus, his brain is seeing your hands up in surrender, so he will be extra surprised when you explode into him. When you strike, use your whole body, rotating your hips and drawing energy from the earth as you push away from it. Imagine your strike going through your target.

Bring him into your personal striking space

When you get to the point where you are striking your attacker, you need to reverse your thinking about keeping him out of your personal space. Now, you need to get into his space in order to disable him. I know you want to keep as far away from him as possible. However, when you are being attacked, the rules change. Now you need to get close to him. It's counterintuitive, I know, but remember you're mad and you need to disable him to get away. Because your arms and legs are probably shorter than the bad guy's, every disabling strike must be executed from a short distance. The closer you are to him, the more powerful and effective your strike will be.

When you come into his space to strike him explosively and with intention, it will most likely be totally unexpected. He will expect you to pull away because he believes you are afraid of getting hurt. But remember, you are expecting to get hurt in order to get away. So, when he pulls you to him, surprise him and explode toward him with elbows or spear hand to his face or a kick to the knee. He's *not* expecting to get hurt and may very well decide that attacking you is not worth the effort. Your unpredictability may make him think twice about his ability to maintain control.

What targets will he give you?

The bad guy may seem invulnerable when you're in a situation with him, but he is not. There are areas of his body that are not protected where, when hit, will blur his vision or make him stumble or fall down. Refocus your energy from where he is grabbing you to what is open to strike. Choose the part of your body closest to his available target and get mad, using power not just to hit it, but to go right through it.

◎ **Eyes** – Use your spear fingers to strike straight into the eye socket. I know it's gross, but it is one of the most effective moves you can make. Remember the hot stove reflex? Well, it is activated when your body is threatened by any type of injury.

When the bad guy sees something coming toward his eyes, his hands will automatically let go of you and rise to protect his face. His head will go up and back. When the eye is injured, vision is lost or blurred, and it's disorienting. Remember the things this guy is capable of and how angry that makes you.

◎ **Nose** – Use your palm strike, the knuckles on the back of your fist, or an elbow from the side to smash into his nose, either from the side or straight on. When the nose is broken, there's lots of blood, vision is blurred, and hands instinctively go to the nose. It's incapacitating. And no, you do not have the power to kill someone by driving their nose into their brain.

◎ **Throat** – If you are in the process of being brutally beaten, abducted, or raped, a strike on the throat can drop a larger, violent attacker. Slam the outside bottom edge of your hand, palm up, across the bad guy's "Adam's apple" and strike through it with all of your might.

◎ **Knees** – Make an imaginary X over your knee with the center of the X on the middle of your kneecap. The lines of the X are about as long as the distance from the tip of your thumb to the tip of your forefinger. The ends of the X are the best places to kick your attacker to disable his knee. You could damage the ligaments which make it difficult for him to walk or stand. Kick with the leg that's closest to him and crash your foot right through one of those points.

◎ **Groin** – You might have been told that men always expect to be hit in the groin and therefore, they "protect" it. Remember, though, that the attacker is expecting a submissive and frightened victim, not the pissed-off, raging woman who has exploded into him. Actually, it is pretty hard to protect that area without leaving other vulnerable areas open. If you are resisting by striking his face, his hands will go up and the groin will be open. If he is using his hands to protect his groin, then his face and throat are vulnerable. He can't protect all of these vulnerable areas at once. So, go for whatever is open. Strike between his legs with maximum force, using your fists, knees, shins, feet, even elbows if you are in the right position. The psychological effects as well as the pain are devastating.

◎ **Shins, ankles, instep** – If you miss his knee, whack into his shin with the side of your foot and run your shoe all the way down the front, ending with a stomp on his ankle, instep, or foot. This may work as a transitional strike, bringing his head down to where you can grab the back of it for a nice knee-strike to the face.

Strike, strike, strike, and continue until escape

With each hit, yell and strike from the center of your being with the intention of inflicting pain so you can escape. Get mad and channel your anger into stopping him from hurting you and anyone else. You may have to hit him many times to escape. He may be on drugs and unable to feel your strikes until he gets his nose broken, eyes poked, or knees blown out. Adrenaline from the stress reaction will provide you with the energy you need.

Try different strikes. Sometimes a person who is very strong in the top half of their body is weak at the bottom. If he doesn't respond to an elbow in the face, then try a kick through his knees. Keep an eye out to see which vulnerable areas are open for business. Continue striking until you can get away. Keep hitting and yelling until you are released.

Remember the power of your voice here. Yell, "NO!" or some other command. Yell your favorite word or two that you use only when you're really angry. Yell "Call 911!" in case there are any bystanders around.

Never give up. Realize that you might have to strike this guy again and again before you disable him, or before he gets the message that you refuse to be an easy target. You will probably get hurt if he hits back, but you are prepared for it. You probably won't even feel it at the time, because adrenaline from the stress reaction will have you totally focused on escape. When you get free and can run, keep going until you reach a safe place. Women have lived through violent situations to go back home to their families. You can survive getting cut with a knife, or shot, to avoid rape. You can survive rape to avoid being murdered. There are no hard and fast rules for what you need to do to survive. Listen to your intuition, and if you choose to resist, do so immediately, loudly, and violently until you are safe.

Practice makes powerful

To be most effective, these strikes need to be practiced. With practice, they become part of your muscle memory that your subconscious will access during a stress reaction. Get a thick cushion from the sofa or a chair and prop it somewhere stable or have someone hold it for you. Imagine the top part as the bad guy's face. Get into your Strong Stance facing your target and practice your palm heel strike. Roll your fingers back, exposing your palm. Feel the energy coming from the earth and through your hips, strike with your palm and yell. Use your hips and entire body to strike, pivoting on the ball of your foot. Go through your target; don't stop at the surface of the cushion.

How about a different strike? Turn your palm down, make a Star Hand, and shoot your elbow into that cushion. Use your hips. You can practice kicking as well. Prop the cushion against a wall. Kick it at knee level with your toes curled back, striking with the ball of your foot. Turn your hips and hit it with the long side of your foot parallel to the ground. Strike fast and with strength. Yell "NO!" loudly each time you hit it. In a real-life situation, each strike must be delivered with explosive movement and the intention to disable, so you can escape.

What about mace?

The beauty of using your body as a weapon is that it is always with you and you are used to using it constantly. Non-lethal weapons available for purchase, such as pepper spray, mace, or stun guns are only good if you are as intimately familiar with them as you are with your hands and feet. If you're going to use these weapons, you have to practice with them until you build muscle memory. You also have to keep them in your hand, since they are useless lying in the bottom of your purse. You will also need to pay attention to factors like the wind when using chemical sprays, or how heavy the bad guy's jacket is for your stun gun to be effective. If you aren't careful, the bad guy can get these weapons from you and use them against you.

Self-defense key chain

I do have one weapon that I carry. It's my Kubotan key chain and the keys on it. Now, I'm NOT talking about the self-defense "tactic" of holding your keys so they protrude through your fingers like little spears for hitting the bad guy if he gets too close. This is, in reality, a bad idea. If you ever had to strike someone using this "weapon", the edges of the keys could sever the tendons in your fingers, making a bloody, painful mess, which is not conducive to self-defense.

My key chain is a five inch long cylinder, sort of shaped like a long lipstick with a key chain on the end. (In fact, they should make this a lipstick instead of just an empty plastic or aluminum tube. Hmm... I'll have to look into this!) I hold my Kubotan cylinder in my hand and swat the bad guy's face with the keys that are dangling from it. I can switch my grip and use the business end of this weapon for striking his soft spots. When it's not in my hand, I keep it in the outside pocket of my purse, easily accessible. The rules for carrying this type of protection are the same for any other non-lethal weapon. Know how to use it (actually, there really is no wrong way, if you're hitting someone with it), keep it handy, and practice using it on a regular basis.

Improvised weapons are always handy

Many weapons are available in your environment. Improvised weapons are everyday items that you can reach which can harm your attacker. They can be divided into five categories of use: items for poking, items for striking harder, items for burning, items for cutting, and items for choking. You can poke an eye out with a pen or your high heel, or use your **cell phone** to strike harder than your bare hand. Fling your coffee or spray hair spray in the bad guy's face, or cut/stab him with scissors. Use your scarf or the cord of your **cell phone** charger to wrap around his neck. Imagine these everyday items as weapons and determine which category would define their use: your umbrella, hairbrush, sunglasses, flashlight, the edge of a book, or perfume spray.

If you get into trouble, use your awareness and look around you to find improvised weapons in the environment. Look up from this book and notice the many things within reach can be used against the bad guy in an emergency. A vase, a lamp, your stapler, or a rolled-up magazine are just some of the things that you could use to defend yourself.

Your Superpower Wallet is getting heavier with your newly learned strategies and tactics. You can resist an attacker, even though you might get hurt. You have thought about what might happen in advance and can react immediately when faced with danger. You are familiar with how to use your personal weapons against a bad guy and have considered where he is most vulnerable. You can strike and you can yell until you escape. You are aware of your environment and can use different items within your reach to help you. Your way of thinking about violence has shifted.

Strength does not come from physical capacity.
It comes from an indomitable will.

– Mahatma Gandhi

Chapter 11
See Your Success
The Power of Visualization

Dream lofty dreams, and as you dream, so shall you become.
Your vision is the promise of what you shall at last unveil.

– John Ruskin

Mental preparation is fundamental for surviving a violent encounter. Fortifying the subconscious with information and practice will help you change your behavior from frozen fear to active resistance in an emergency. Now let's add affirmations and visualizations of successful resistance and escape to your Superpower Wallet.

Positive statements aid your subconscious

You can effect a positive change in your thinking habits with affirmations. An affirmation is simply a positive statement specifically worded to describe your completed goal. It's sort of like a script for your subconscious. Now, I'm not talking about mindlessly repeating some banality like "I'm getting better every day in every way." No, I mean words you can think and say that can change patterns of negative thought, those old counterproductive tapes that keep playing in your subconscious which affect your actions.

Here's how it works. Your brain, particularly your subconscious, is like an actor in a play. It will read and act out whatever script it is given. It responds to instructions and direction. All through this book, we've been working on programming your subconscious with effective safety habits and skills. Affirmations are just you rewriting the script of how you think, which will supplement the skills and habits you've learned. These positive images and thoughts will help guide you to safety in a dangerous situation. Create a script where you are successfully accomplishing your goals and it will effectively delete the old scripts of negative, self-defeating images. Honestly, your brain does not know the difference, so give it something good to work with. When you change how you talk to yourself, you will behave differently.

It's best if you can write your own script. How do you want to feel? Find a negative thought that is hindering you and choose a positive one to replace it. Where do you want to be? Picture your goal accomplished. The main rules are that you start with "I am," and keep it short, specific, and positive. Speak in the present tense using action verbs ending in –ing, and lace it with the emotion you would like to be feeling once the goal is completed. You can also use the rhythmic rhyming type of affirmation, which is easy to remember and just plain fun to say. It doesn't even matter if you believe it to be true at this time. Your subconscious will sort it all out for you.

Get a little notebook and write down your affirmations, the script for your subconscious, each morning when you wake up and each evening before going to bed. Say them out loud as you are writing them. Bring them into your consciousness when meditating. Feel the emotion they generate. Write the really juicy ones on cards and place them in spots where you can see them during the day.

To get you started, I've come up with some safety affirmations of my own. Feel free to use them until you have your own list.

I have the right to defend myself and the ability to succeed.

I am enforcing my boundaries with awareness and assertion.

I am aware of my surroundings.

Relax, relax, to accomplish the max.

As I watch how things unfold, I am centered and controlled.

I breathe fully and calmly, relaxing my body.

The feeling of fear will help me get clear.

Intuition starts my ignition.

I am paying attention to my feelings and perceptions about the world around me.

When I feel fear, I get into gear.

I am successfully recognizing the difference between the guys who will hurt me and guys who will respect my wishes.

I am standing tall and taking responsibility for my personal safety.

I am speaking strongly and assertively to protect myself and my family.

I am confidently saying no to requests that are not in line with my highest priorites.

I am entitled to my own opinion and am comfortable disagreeing with others.

I own my personal power, honoring it, and using it for good.

I am enjoying my strong body and its ability to be responsive to my needs.

I am strong in tough situations.

I am adapting to the unpredictable with speed and action.

I am a courageous, risk-taking woman warrior.

I can forcefully strike and escape when I like.

I resist and resist, always persist.

I am powerfully defending myself outside of my comfort zone.

I am in control and this guy's gonna roll.

I have the right and responsibility to express my anger in an emergency situation.

I am totally committing to my best effort with 100% confidence in victory.

OK, I can just hear what you're saying now. Something along the lines of "Horse puckey, this is not even close to true!" Well, maybe it's not true right this second, but you are not lying to yourself when you make a statement that is not totally true now but can be fully true in the future. Affirmations are for direction. Even if you fall short of your affirmations of greatness, you will still end up closer to your goal than if you had set lower sights or had no direction at all. Each time your repeat a positive statement about your safety, you are rewriting the script of your subconscious, providing valuable direction.

Make sure, too, that you double-check your beliefs about yourself. Take a second and examine how valid your belief is, for example, that you can't defend yourself. What proof do you really have? And how old is this "proof?" Maybe there were a couple of times you did not stand up for yourself in the past. That was when you didn't have the information that you have today. Yesterday's actions don't always have to repeat themselves. You are rewriting your script. The truth is that you have the tools in your Superpower Wallet to defend yourself. However, to create a more direct route for the brain to access during a stress reaction, you need to use visualization.

Visualization creates success

You can replace the negative self-talk with positive affirmations. However, to really seal in the type of direction the brain will access during a stress reaction, you need to use visualization. Visualization creates a mental movie of you successfully avoiding or surviving a violent encounter. In this movie, not only are you writing the script, you set the scene and cast yourself in the lead role, using all of your senses to harness the creative power of the subconscious.

Visualization has been used by professional athletes with great success. Elite athletes achieve their goals by visualizing themselves succeeding. Olympic skier Julia Mancuso created a poster of herself winning gold medals when she was just twelve years old. It stayed up on her wall for years, effectively training her subconscious. For peak performance before every race, she inspects the course, then visualizes where she will turn and what her timing will be. By the time she gets to the start gate, she clears her mind of everything else but the race, relying on her muscle memory of practiced moves and her visualization of the best way to get down the hill. If visualization works to achieve gold medals, it can also work for successful self-defense.

Your brain uses the same process whether performing a task or visualizing it. Your subconscious does not know the difference between something you vividly imagine and true reality. One of the basic laws of the mind is that whenever your conscious and subconscious are in conflict, your subconscious invariably wins. During a stress reaction, your brain goes straight to the subconscious for direction and guidance. If you create a movie of what you really want to do in a particular situation, your subconscious mind will accept it as valid. Once an idea has been accepted by the subconscious mind, it remains there until it is replaced by another idea. The longer it is held and the more it is accessed, the more it tends to become a fixed habit or thought pattern. This is how habits of action are formed, both good and bad. Visualizing successful self-defense can take advantage of these laws to keep you safe.

Try this at home

Grab your partner and practice visualization for self-defense. Hand this book to your partner. Have them read the visualization exercise below (in italics) out loud as you sit in a quite place with your eyes closed. Relax and follow their instructions. You can also read this exercise into a voice recorder and play it back as you sit and listen.

Close your eyes and take a deep breath, drawing the air deep into your belly. Hold your breath for a count of three and then breathe out, allowing yourself to relax. Imagine your body is covered with a warm glow of relaxation. Breathe and relax. Open your eyes as you breathe in again and when you breathe out close your eyes again, going deeper into relaxation. Repeat this phrase to yourself. "I have the right to defend myself and the ability to succeed." You know that this is true anywhere you may be. You are practicing awareness wherever you are. Your intuition is sharp and perceptive and you are listening to it. You know how to defend your boundary, have prepared mentally, and can fight through physical discomfort and fatigue until you are safe.

Now imagine yourself in a place where you feel threatened. Possibly it's in the parking lot at night, heading toward your car, and seeing a shady character hanging around. Perhaps it's in your home as you're getting ready for bed and you hear a strange noise downstairs. Pick a place and concentrate on it. See the images, recognize the familiar smells of that place, and hear the background noises. You are aware and alert. Check in with your feelings of fear and discomfort.

Breathe to get calm. You are aware and notice the details of where you are. You smell the oily car smell of the parking lot or, if you're at home, taste the peppermint flavor of the toothpaste you used as you were getting ready for bed. If you are at home, you hear a noise sounding like glass breaking, but you're not sure. In the parking lot, you see a man walking toward you in the next lane of cars as you are loading your packages into your car. You make observations about the situation and know that you are not paranoid but are prepared. You are checking your intuition and are getting some bad vibes. You are paying close attention to these signals. You are making plans to defend yourself as you confront the intruder. Imagine your boundary around you. Notice how you know exactly how you are going to strike him if he does attack. You are standing strong and stating clearly what you want this intruder to do in a calm and serious tone. Your body language totally supports your confident commands. Perhaps the intruder gets frustrated and calls you a name. You stand your ground in Strong Stance, physically and mentally. You feel fear, but it is driving you to calm, focused confrontation. Notice that the intruder is backing away, maybe you still hear him yelling, but going out of the parking lot or out of your house. Notice how calm, focused, and confident you are while still aware of this guy and where he is going. Notice how the perception of being rude is no longer a concern. Notice how proud you are that you successfully maintained your awareness and remained calm and confident during the entire situation. Let that scene fade away and breathe. Breathe deeply in and out, going deeper into relaxation.

Imagine going back to the scenario in the parking lot or in your bedroom at night, after you defined your boundary. Even though you have stated clearly and loudly what you want the intruder to do, he advances and invades your boundary. The natural fear response is replaced by an overwhelming focus that is strong and intense. You are breathing and present. You feel him grab you. Feel yourself harness your fear, get angry, and resist immediately and loudly. Feel your elbow slice his face and your foot blast through his knee. The harder he struggles to control you, the more violent your strikes become. Your strikes are hard and fast and land exactly where you want them: his nose, his throat, his groin. Every strike is causing damage. You may be tired or injured and you can see blood. Imagine *looking around the area for something that you can use as a weapon. Imagine grabbing that object. He tries for you again and somehow you have reached your **cell phone** or a lamp nearby. You slam your new-found weapon into his face and neck. You continue slamming until the intruder is stunned enough that you can run to safety. Imagine where that would be and how you would get there. You arrive safely and call the police and they come to help. You tell them you feared for your life and you successfully defended yourself because you had no other choice. Visualize yourself using deep-breathing techniques to reduce your stress level. Notice how you feel so proud that you protected yourself in a violent situation. Now you know that you have the right to defend yourself and the ability to succeed.*

As you open your eyes, know that you always carry with you the strength, focus, and control you have just experienced.

Now switch places and have your partner relax and sit quietly while you read the exercise. Create your own movie scripts where you successfully hear and act on your intuition, stand firm, say no, resist, and escape.

Arm your subconscious

The unknown is fuel for fear. By learning, thinking about, and implementing the self-defense techniques and options in this book, you can transform your fear into action. When your Superpower Wallet is full, your subconscious brain will have something to refer to when it's the only thing running the show. This is still no guarantee that you won't get hurt, but you increase the odds of escaping and surviving.

Be aware of violence in the media. With your newfound knowledge, look at different violent situations you see on television or in the newspaper from the point of view of the victim. Imagine what you could do in different crime situations. Think about how you would deal with the fear. Imagine what you would say and what actions you could take. What avenues of escape are available and where would you end up if you went that way? What strikes could you employ and what targets does the bad guy make available to you? How might you be injured? Even though you might be injured, how will you act? Most importantly, how could you have prevented this encounter in the first place?

Anytime that you can imagine yourself escaping and winning in a violent situation, your subconscious will be better prepared for a violent encounter. When you're out and about, be aware of the people you see when you're on the street, in the subway, or moving through any marginal area. Imagine what you would do if someone suddenly came toward you in a threatening manner. What options would you use that are in your Superpower Wallet? Imagine yourself executing those options successfully to avoid or escape danger.

Close your eyes and imagine your Superpower Wallet, now quite full of information, options, and exercises that you can use to keep yourself safe. Add the power of visualization and practice affirmations to strengthen your response to violence. Work with a partner on a regular basis to create safety habits that increase your control, focus, and power.

I've dreamt in my life dreams that have stayed with me ever after, and changed my ideas; they've gone through and through me, like wine through water, and altered the color of my mind.

– Emily Bronte

Chapter 12

You Are Superwoman

The fish only knows that it lives in the water, after it is already on the river bank. Without our awareness of another world out there, it would never occur to us to change.

– Source unknown

It's a different world now. In this new world you're aware of violence, but it's like the flu. You don't want an encounter with it, but it is out there. Like violence in our world, the flu is everywhere. However, because you eat healthy and employ preventive health measures, the "bug" generally passes you by. Sometimes, though, you catch the flu, despite all of your precautions. You know that some people can die from the flu. Chances are you won't die, however, because you know how to take care of yourself when you're sick. You know where to go and where not to go, how to treat your body, and what measures are necessary to get yourself healthy again. Sometimes you have to employ drugs as weapons to fight it off. You can fight it off because you know what to do. You don't go around fearful of dying from the flu, but you do know what it can do to you and what you can do to combat it. In the same way, you are aware of violence and now have some options of how to deal with it.

Take responsibility for your own safety

I would like to see you take responsibility for your own safety, just like you take responsibility for your own health. Employ preventive measures against crime. Practice breathing and awareness in every possible situation. Know how your intuition speaks to you and act on it immediately when it sends you signals of danger. Redefine your emotional boundary to include only the good guys. Defend your strong boundary with loud and clear communication. Have a plan for escape from your home and from anybody who might get within your personal boundary. Practice breaking away from a grab and striking an assailant. Train your subconscious so it knows what to do. When you can protect yourself, you are protecting your family and the people who care about you as well. You are Superwoman.

You also send a clear message to the bad guys that neither offensive nor criminal behavior will be tolerated. Speak up when you hear a joke that's offensive to women and let people know that it is not acceptable. Inform guys who harass you on the street that their conduct is an insult to you, can be downright scary to other women, and it must stop. Let the guy who is harassing you at work know loud and clear that his behavior is inappropriate and offensive. Document all instances of harassment and report them. You can become a hard target. When enough of us make it difficult for the bad guy to commit crimes against women, the world will be a much better place. You are Superwoman.

You have the tools to keep yourself safe

Take out your Superpower Wallet and feel its weight. It should feel much fuller and heavier than when you first created it. Make sure that you take it out often to review the contents. Share what you have in it with your friends, both male and female. Practice the exercises with them. Many of these concepts are useful in other stressful situations besides self-defense. Take what you now know and use it to enrich your life.

It's dark out. You're working late and you've got to get from your building to your car parked in the lot. You have so many things on your mind. But, before you leave the building, you stop, take a breath or two, and table any thoughts dealing with the past or the future. Your key is in your hand and you can easily manage whatever else you're carrying. As you walk out of the building, you calmly note that everyone is moving as they should be and there is nothing unusual. You see a man walking by himself in the next lane. You imagine what you would do if he came into your lane. You stand a little straighter and imagine how you would verbally warn him that he is not welcome or wanted within your boundary space. You see that there are other people in the parking lot who could hear you if you had to tell him louder. He stays in the next lane. You feel confident that you could communicate what you need and, if things went bad, you could use your fear to energize yourself into action. You arrive at your car, load your briefcase or packages, lock the doors, buckle up, smile, and go.

For what is done or learned by one class of women becomes, by virtue of their common womanhood, the property of all women.

– Elizabeth Blackwell

Afterword

Congratulations! You have arrived at the conclusion of this book and are ready to proceed with implementing strategies that will make your life safer, more peaceful, and productive. You have committed a bold act by choosing to be responsible for your own safety. I thank you for traveling with me this far and commend you on your desire to live a safer life.

I know that you probably won't be able to implement or even digest every strategy the first time through. After all, this is life-changing stuff! I hope, though, that you will take time out of your busy day in order to make these safety strategies a habit. Maybe even take one week to just practice paying attention, one week to fortify the defenses of your home, one week to especially listen to your intuition. And every day, practice standing with your shoulders rolled back and imagine what you would do if you were in a situation where you needed to kick in your self-defense skills.

Fortunately, for the two of us, our journey does not have to end here. If you got this book from one of my seminars, I'll be in touch with you regularly with even more suggestions of how you can learn to live a safer life. If you did not get this book from me, then take the initiative to get in touch with me on my website, www.DEFYTheBadGuy.com. It's very much in your interest, whether you simply want additional safety suggestions or whether you want me to come to speak to a group of your colleagues or club members.

But whether I can help you or not, be sure to drop me a line and tell me about your experiences using the strategies in this book. Or better yet, let me know how you defied a bad guy in any way! Share your own tips and information so that I may be able to make the following editions of this book better. I am by no means at the end of my learning journey and it is my desire to figure out all that I can do to assist women like you to create the safest life possible. In fact, I would be tickled pink to learn these things from you, the person who now has the ability to equip herself with effective safety strategies. You can find my email, website, and address on the back page of this book. I look forward to hearing from you soon!

Success in Safety,

Julie Greene

About the Author

Julie Greene is the founder and author of the DEFY the Bad Guy book and seminars, teaching women powerful and practical self-defense strategies. Her passion for teaching and her search for powerful and effective ways to defend yourself have come together to help women who want to be safe.

She is a head instructor and has earned three black belts in the Korean martial art TaeKwonDo, and is a black belt in Combat Hapkido. She is a certified R.A.D. Systems instructor, and is a licensed instructor for the International Police Defensive Tactics Institute. She has studied and reached instructor level in the Combat Hapkido Ground Survival Program and the Anatomical Targeting Strategies Program. She is a member of the Association for Women's Self-Defense Advancement.

Julie graduated cum laude with a Bachelor's degree from the College of William and Mary in Williamsburg, Virginia.

When she's not practicing her strikes and kicks, she is a homeschool teacher to her son, Morgan, and together they travel around the world with her husband, George. Their two cats, Shadow and Smoky, stay at home.

Resources

WEBSITES

Crime Statistics

Sexual Assault Statistics: www.rainn.org
General Crime Statistics: www.ojp.usdoj.gov/bjs

Domestic Violence

National Domestic Violence Hotline: www.ndvh.org 1-800-799-SAFE
National Coalition Against Domestic Violence: www.ncadv.org
National Network to End Domestic Violence: www.nnedv.org
Break The Cycle: www.breakthecycle.org

Drugs

Club Drugs: www.clubdrugs.gov
US Drug Enforcement Administration: www.usdoj.gov/dea

Home Safety

Home Safety Council: www.homesafetycouncil.org
National Safety Council: www.nsc.org

Identity Theft

Free Credit Report: www.annualcreditreport.com
Federal Trade Commission: www.ftc.gov/bcp/edu/microsites/idtheft
OnGuard Online: www.onguardonline.gov

Legal and Legislative Information

National Center for Victims of Crime: www.ncvc.org
FindLaw: www.findlaw.com
National Crime Prevention Council: www.ncpc.org

Sexual Assault and Rape

Rape, Abuse, and Incest National Network: www.rainn.org

RAINN Hotline: 1-800-656-HOPE
Rape Treatment: www.911rape.org
National Sexual Violence Resource Center: www.nsvrc.org – call for
the sexual assault crisis center in your area
Security On Campus, Inc.: www.securityoncampus.org
National Registry of Sex Offenders: www.nsopr.gov
No Nonsense Self-Defense: www.nononsenseselfdefense.com
My Mobile Witness: www.mymobilewitness.com

Sexual Harassment and Stalking

The US Equal Employment Opportunity Commission: www.eeoc.gov
Sexual Harassment Support: www.sexualharassmentsupport.org
Stalking Resource Center: www.ncvc.org/src
Stalking Victims Sanctuary: www.stalkingvictims.com

Survivors of Child Abuse

Survivors of Incest Anonymous: http://www.siawso.org
Adult Children of Alcoholics: www.adultchildren.org

Violence Against Women

Women's Legal Defense & Education Fund: www.legalmomentum.org
Office on Violence Against Women: www.ovw.usdoj.gov/

Self-Defense

Combat Hapkido: www.dsihq.com
R.A.D. Systems: www.rad-systems.com

Travel

State Department: www.travel.state.gov
Transportation Security Administraion: www.tsa.gov
Airline Seat Maps: www.seatguru.com
Ground Transportation information: www.ihatetaxis.com

RECOMMENDED READING

Steering by Starlight by Martha Beck. Rodale Books, 2008.
www.marthabeck.com

Her Wits About Her: Self-Defense Success Stories by Women by Denise Caignon. HarperCollins, 1987.

The Gift of Fear by Gavin De Becker. Little, Brown, and Company, 1997. www.gavindebecker.com

Fear Less by Gavin De Becker. Little Brown, and Company, 2002. www.gavindebecker.com

The Bulletproof Mind (What it Takes to Win Violent Encounters... And After) by Lt. Col. Dave Grossman. Calibre Press, 1996. www.warriorscience.com

Total Relaxation: Healing Practices for Body, Mind, and Spirit by John R. Harvey, Ph.D. Kodansha International 1998.

Strong on Defense by Sanford Strong. Atria, 1997. www.sgtstrong.com

A New Earth: Awakening to Your Life's Purpose by Eckhart Tolle. Walker and Co., 2005. www.eckharttolle.com

Mental Training for Peak Performance by Steven Underleider, Ph.D. Rodale, 2005.

EASY ORDER FORM

E-mail orders: Orders@DEFYTheBadGuy.com

Telephone orders: call +1-757-856-9518
Have your credit card ready.

Postal orders: Julie Greene Safety Solutions
P.O. Box 1523
Hampton VA 23661 USA

Please send me _____ copy(ies) of this book. I understand that if I am not 100% satisfied with this book, I may return it and get a free refund – no questions asked.

See www.DEFYTheBadGuy.com for free information on upcoming CDs, courses, Speaking Seminars, and Consulting.

Please send me **FREE** information on:

☐Other Educational Materials ☐ Speaking & Seminar Dates ☐ Coaching

Name: _____

Address: _____

City _____ State/Province _____ Postal Code: _____

Telephone: _____

Email: _____

Payment: ☐Check: Credit Card: ☐ Visa ☐ MasterCard

Card number: _____

Name on card: _____

Expiration date: (mm/yy) _____

Shipping by air: U.S.: $4.00 for first book and $2.00 for each additional book. International: $9.00 for first book and $5.00 for each additional book (estimate).

EASY ORDER FORM

E-mail orders: Orders@DEFYTheBadGuy.com

Telephone orders: call **+1-757-856-9518**
Have your credit card ready.

Postal orders: Julie Greene Safety Solutions
P.O. Box 1523
Hampton VA 23661 USA

Please send me _____ copy(ies) of this book. I understand that if I am not 100% satisfied with this book, I may return it and get a free refund – no questions asked.

See www.DEFYTheBadGuy.com for free information on upcoming CDs, courses, Speaking Seminars, and Consulting.

Please send me **FREE** information on:

☐Other Educational Materials   ☐ Speaking & Seminar Dates   ☐ Coaching

Name: _____

Address: _____

City _____ State/Province _____ Postal Code: _____

Telephone: _____

Email: _____

Payment: ☐Check: Credit Card: ☐ Visa ☐ MasterCard

Card number: _____

Name on card: _____

Expiration date: (mm/yy) _____

Shipping by air: U.S.: $4.00 for first book and $2.00 for each additional book. International: $9.00 for first book and $5.00 for each additional book (estimate).

CPSIA information can be obtained at www.ICGtesting.com
Printed in the USA
LVOW131043101012

302262LV00003B/154/P